# LAST OF THE RED HOT CATS

## THE LIVES OF THE CIVILIAN GRUMMAN F8F BEARCATS

ROBERT C. "BOB" KENNEDY

**Front cover image**: C/n D.1262, N700A, the Last of the Red Hot Cats. (Doug Slowiak)

**Title page image**: C/n D.1053 and c/n D.1181 on display at the 1967 Reno Air Races where neither would race. (Emil Strasser)

**Contents page image:** C/Nn D.902 N212KA was one of the few Bearcats used for aerial survey work. (Jerry Liang)

**Back cover image**: C/N. D.1181, N148F in a beautiful Grumman Hawk paint scheme. (Russ Hiatt)

**Dedication**

This book is dedicated to all of the United States Navy and United States Marine Corps pilots who flew Grumman's Hot Rod, "Job Well Done." Also, to the following great historians and photographers: William T. Larkins, Dusty Carter, Malcolm Gougon, Larry Smalley, Dick Phillips, Russ Hiatt, Al Hansen, Geoff Goodall and Emil Strasser. They will always be with us.

**Acknowledgements**

Gerald Liang, Nicholas A. "Nick" Veronico, Doug Slowiak, Dan Hagedorn, Jim Dunn, Roger Cain, Jay Sherlock, Brian Baker, Jay Miller, Blanche Snyder CNO, Roger Keeney, Bruce Lockwood, Ms H.J. Schonenberg and Lois Lovisolo of Grumman Aircraft Corporation Public Affairs, Ms Carrie LaFollette of FAA Registration Branch, Steve Hinton of the Air Museum, and the late Ed Maloney. To my children, Courtney, Brian and Jason, thank you for putting up with my plane craziness.

Published by Key Books
An imprint of Key Publishing Ltd
PO Box 100
Stamford
Lincs PE9 1XQ

www.keypublishing.com

The right of Robert C. "Bob" Kennedy to be identified as the author of this book has been asserted in accordance with the Copyright, Designs and Patents Act 1988 Sections 77 and 78.



Typeset by SJmagic DESIGN SERVICES, India.

# CONTENTS

# ABBREVIATIONS AND TERMS

| | |
|---|---|
| **AGL** | Above ground level |
| **A&P** | Airframe and powerplant |
| **AOV** | Average order value |
| **BAR** | Bureau of Aeronautics Representative |
| **BuAer** | Bureau of Aeronautics United States Navy |
| **BuNo** | Bureau of Aeronautics number, military serial number |
| **CASU** | Combat Aircraft Service Unit |
| **C/N** | Construction number |
| **CVG** | Carrier Air Group |
| **DBA** | Doing business as |
| **DMG** | Damaged, airframe received enough damage as to make it unflyable |
| **DNF** | Did not finish |
| **DNQ** | Did not qualify |
| **DNR** | Did not race |
| **DNS** | Did not start |
| **FA** | Fiscal Assets Department, United States Navy |
| **FAA** | Federal Aviation Administration |
| **FASRON** | Fleet Aircraft Service Squadron |
| **FLEET** | The collective aircraft/ships in use by the United States Navy |
| **FLYABLE** | Airframe is complete and flown on a regular basis |
| **Hrs** | Hours/time flown or run, airframe or engine |
| **HYBRID** | Composite airframe, a combination of airframe parts or engines |
| **IFR** | Instrument Flight Rules |
| **Kts** | Knots |
| **MDAP** | Mutual Defense Assistance Program |
| **MCAS** | Marine Corps Air Station |
| **M&S** | Material Service Division |
| **N#** | Civil registration number |
| **NAF** | Naval Air Facility |
| **NAS** | Naval Air Station |
| **NATC** | Naval Air Test Center |
| **NART** | Naval Air Reserve Training |
| **NARTU** | Naval Air Reserve Training Unit |
| **NTSB** | National Transportation Safety Administration |
| **O&R** | Overhaul and Repair Department |
| **OVC** | Other valuable consideration |
| **PIC** | Pilot in command |
| **POOL** | Group of aircraft assigned to station waiting delivery to fleet squadrons/units |
| **REBUILDABLE** | Airframe damaged but by current standards can be returned to flight |
| **RESTORATION** | Airframe has been damaged or in need of overhaul due to high engine/airframe hours and is being repaired or rebuilt |
| **RETIREMENT** | Withdrawn from further use |
| **RPM** | Revolutions per minute |
| **SMOH** | Since major overhaul |
| **STORED** | Airframe in storage in an unflyable state, but complete |
| **STRICKEN** | Removed from inventory |
| **T/O** | Take-off |
| **TT** | Total Time, accumulated hours on airframe or engine since new |
| **VFR** | Visual flight rules |
| **VSI** | Vertical speed indicator |
| **W/O** | Written off. Airframe destroyed. However, some pieces may still exist or have been used in another airframe but are not listed as part of the original airframe construction number (c/n) |

F8F-2 c/n 1261, BuNo 122708 was the last United States Navy Bearcat to be built. (Emil Strasser)

# Chapter 1

# THE BEGINNING

When the last F8F Bearcat rolled off the Grumman assembly line at Bethpage, New York (NY), in May 1949, it ended a line of truly remarkable naval propeller-driven fighter aircraft that had begun with the FF-1 "Flying Barrels" in 1931. The Bearcat was one of the last production propeller-driven, single-seat fighters to be built in the United States. The Vought CORSAIR was still in production. Its replacement, the jet-powered F9F Panther, entered fleet service the same month, clearly signaling the Bearcat's days were numbered.

*Left*: Grumman XFF-1 BuNo 8878 (Model G-5) was the first of Grumman's "Flying Barrel" fighters under test at Naval Air Station (NAS) Anacostia, Virginia, in 1932. It was destroyed in March 1937 as a result of fuel starvation. (Grumman Corporation)

*Opposite*: The next step towards the perfect fighter was the F3F-2 (G-19), BuNo 0994 of Marine Fighter Squadron Two, VMF-2, at Bakersfield, California, in 1939. (Russ Hiatt)

C
2·MF·15
0994
3F-2
U.S.M.

*Left*: Grumman Model G-22 c/n 355, NR1050, civil demonstrator of the F3F flown by Major Al Williams (Ret.) as *Gulfhawk II* for Gulf Oil Co. It is now part of the National Air and Space Museum collection. (Grumman Corp)

*Opposite*: First XF4F-5 BuNo 1846 (G-36) Wildcat illustrating progress toward a modern carrier fighter. (Grumman Corp)

1846    XF4F-5
U.S.NAVY

The Bearcat's big brother was the F6F (G-50) Hellcat. Bearcats are smaller than Hellcats and were not intended to replace Hellcats. The F8Fs were built for the mission of lightweight interceptors/fighters. Number 3 is an F6F-5, BuNo 78728, assigned to the Naval Reserve Unit at NAS Los Alamitos, California, and photographed at the 1947 Cleveland National Air Races. (Emil Strasser)

Bearcat number one XF8F-1 (G-58), BuNo 90460, photographed 22 days after its first flight on August 31, 1944. It was written off in a crash in March 1945. Flight trials would reveal the need to increase the size of the vertical tail and the addition of a dorsal spine. Both prototypes were the only F8Fs to have Pratt & Whitney R-2800-22W engines. (Grumman Corp)

## Development

The F8F design began in early 1943 when the United States was not winning the war in the Pacific. The United States Navy realized it would need a fighter that could outperform the newer Japanese fighters then entering service. The formidable F6F Hellcat was just making its combat debut. Grumman's Chief Engineer William Schwendler believed any replacement for the F6F Hellcat should be fast and versatile, both ideas he put into the design of the F8F. The F8F was of typical Grumman design as it was rugged, innovative, and well-armed with four 0.50 guns; it differed from previous Grumman fighters by being unbelievably fast. It has been said the Grumman design team built the smallest airframe around the most dependable radial engine of the time, the Pratt & Whitney (P&W) R-2800 Double Wasp. Although the F8F was built as a fighter, it was not a replacement for the F6F. Bearcats were physically smaller than their predecessors and intended to be flown from the Navy's fast carriers. They were known as lightweight fast interceptors, the first and last of the breed for the United States Navy.

The first F8F flew for the first time on August 31, 1944. Despite the loss of the first prototype in March 1945, the United States Navy ordered the F8F into production.

Besides its high-powered performance, the F8F was also innovative in other ways. The F8F introduced the first full-blown or bubble canopy on United States Naval aircraft and one of the first high-pressure hydraulic systems (1,500psi), which later led to problems in both squadron and civil service. The aircraft had jettisonable wing tips; it was stubby, to fit more aircraft on the smaller fast carriers, and was short-coupled with a high roll rate.

Another innovation introduced on the Dash 2 was the unique Automatic Engine Control (AEC). This system regulated the throttle and variable speed supercharger. It was designed as a time-saving device that would allow the pilot more free time to fly by replacing the separate throttle and supercharger controls, combining them into one unit. This system was also to prove troublesome in both military and civil Cats. With all of the new features, plus the fact that the F8F was the most powerful and fastest prop fighter of its day, it could be a handful to fly.

*Opposite*: Number one developmental XF8F-1, BuNo 90437, photographed on April 20, 1945, about three months after its first flight. Note the taller tail and dorsal spine. It was now powered by the Pratt & Whitney R-2800-34W engine that would be used on production F8F-1s. The 23 developmental XF8F-1s were used by the Navy for a variety of tests. Two of these, c/n D.10, BuNo 90446 and c/n D.18, BuNo 90454, would survive testing and were civil registered. BuNo 90437 ended its days as a static test airframe. (Grumman Corp)

*Right*: The fifth developmental XF8F-1, BuNo 90441, photographed on March 20, 1945, showing the wing fold and close cowling of the R-2800-34W engine. The F8Fs' squat stance is apparent from this angle. BuNo 90441 was the second F8F to roll off the production line. All previous Bearcats had been built in the Grumman experimental shop. (Grumman Corp)

Upon entering fleet service, the F8F soon gained the reputation of being a "Red Hot Cat" to fly due to its combination of a big engine and its short-coupled airframe. This combination produced great speed and outstanding maneuverability. In 1946, a stock F8F-1 flown by Lt. Cdr. Davenport set a new time-to-climb record of 10,000ft in 94 seconds after making a 115ft take-off run.

There were a number of fatal crashes caused by this combination and by engine and system problems that added to the Bearcat's "Red Hot" reputation. From early 1945 to late 1952, there were approximately 270 accidents that resulted in heavy damage or write-offs.

To be fair to the F8F, most were landing accidents, deck strikes, a few mid-air collisions, poor fuel management and, with veteran pilots moving up to jets, a new crop of young naval aviators lacking experience.

The issues with Bearcat systems were mostly corrected shortly before F8Fs left the fleet. As with anything troublesome, people only remember the bad. Later, when flown by the United States Marines as close-air-support trainers, a few F8Fs shed their wings. This resulted in a controversial fix using spar caps that only added to its reputation as a killer. There will be more on the spar-cap fix later. After 1,263 F8Fs and two G-58s were built, production ended.

*Left*: BuNo 90441 side view highlights the sleek and clean lines of the Bearcat. In 1946, this aircraft would be converted into an F8F-1P photo-reconnaissance model for testing different camera installations. (Grumman Corp)

*Opposite*: The X7 was the seventh developmental X8F-1, BuNo 90443. It is shown testing long-range, 300-gallon drop tanks on November 27, 1945, during acceptance trials. These tests identified directional stability and control problems while carrying external stores. This would plague the F8F throughout its service life. Lyle Shelton used A-4 drop tanks of a similar size in the 1971 US Cup Race and it took all the horsepower and his flying skills to keep the plane on the racecourse. (Grumman Corp)

X
7
G-22485
11-27-45

## Models and Military Service

Two XF8F-1 prototypes (BuNo 90460 and 90461) with R-2800-22W engines were produced followed by 23 XF8F-1 pre-production or developmental aircraft (BuNo 90437–90459). These differed from the prototypes by having R-2800-34W engines and a dorsal fin plus larger horizontal tails. Production models were F8F-1s and F8F-1Bs with cannon armament. The F8F-1Ns were radar-equipped night fighters. These were followed by improved F8F-2s with taller vertical tails, dorsal fin, R-2800-30W engines and 20mm cannons. The Dash-2N was a night fighter with an AN/APS-19 radar, while the F8F-2P was equipped for aerial reconnaissance.

*Left*: Excellent factory delivery photo of F8F-2, BuNo 122689, showing the elegant lines of a true fighter. Bearcats possessed great speed, fantastic maneuverability, good all-around vision, and four 20mm cannons providing a lethal punch. (Grumman Corp)

*Opposite*: Out to the fleet, F8F-1 BuNo 94795, on its way to the Pool at NAS Norfolk, Virginia. By 1949, there were 24 squadrons flying Bearcats with the United States Navy. Notice all the Bearcats on the ramp behind BuNo 94795. This photo was taken at the Bethpage, New York, factory. After Navy service this -1 went to the French Air Force and then to Thailand. (Grumman Corp)

VF-742 aboard the USS *Midway* in August 1952, with F8F-2P BuNo 121611 (E212) and brothers preparing for launch. (William T. Larkins Collection)

A fine photo of F8F-2 BuNo 121546 of VF-72 showing fleet markings on a clean-looking Bearcat. L-222 would survive its naval service and was scrapped at NAS North Island, California. (William T. Larkins Collection)

F8F-2 BuNo 121701 from VF-152 at San Francisco, California, on October 30, 1949. It had been aboard the USS *Antietam*. Two Bearcats from this same BuNo group, 121699 and 121707, would make it to the civil registry. (William T. Larkins Collection)

Like most military services, the United States Navy has always been eager to show the taxpayers where their money goes. The Bearcat was flown and demonstrated by the Navy's Flight Demonstration Squadron, the Blue Angels, from 1946 to mid-1949. Blue Angels' aircraft #1 BuNo 94996 is shown at the National Air Races, Cleveland, Ohio, in September 1946. (Emil Strasser)

Bearcats served with 24 United States Navy fleet squadrons, starting with the first operational squadron, VF-19, on May 21, 1945. Bearcats also served three Marine training squadrons before being sent to the reserves once jets were introduced to the fleet.[1] The United States Navy Flight Demonstration Team, the Blue Angels, flew Bearcats from 1946–49.

The year 1953 saw the beginning of the final withdrawal of F8Fs from service by both regular and reserve squadrons. Records show the last squadrons to fly F8Fs were reserve squadrons VF-921 and VF-859, recording flights in January 1953. Some remained in utility squadrons and test units until late 1956 when the last of the Red Hot Cats were stricken from United States Navy inventory.

---

1 See Steve Ginter's excellent book *Grumman F8F Bearcat* for a complete military service history.

After the Blue Angels traded in their Bearcats for F9Fs, Bearcat F8F-1B BuNo 95487 was used as an antagonist during their routine. *Beetle Bomb* is seen at NAS Alameda, California, in late 1949. (William T. Larkins)

The end of the line for F8F-2D BuNo 121782 of Utility Squadron Two (VU-2). It was photographed on April 9, 1958, at NAS Litchfield Park, Arizona, after it was withdrawn from use. Utility Squadron Bearcats were some of the last to see active United States Navy service. This aircraft did not survive and is presumed to have been scrapped along with hundreds of others at Litchfield and NAS North Island, California. (Brian Baker)

As Bearcats were withdrawn from service, they were placed into storage at either Naval Air Facility (NAF) Litchfield Park in Arizona (AZ) or Naval Air Station (NAS) North Island in San Diego, California (CA).

Having never fired its guns in defense of the United States, the F8F was deemed unsuitable for combat during the Korean conflict (1950–53). This was partly due to its inability to act as a fighter-bomber in a similar way to the F4U Corsair. The F8Fs always had a slight instability problem when carrying external stores.

Of those placed in storage, some Bearcats were sold or given to France as early as 1951 under Mutual Defense Assistance Programs (MDAP). This number was approximately 140 F8F-1s and -1Bs. Some were passed to the Vietnamese when France withdrew from Vietnam. Another batch of 120 F8F-1s and -1Bs went to Thailand under the same type of transaction. The rest are presumed scrapped.

The Navy put some 50 F8F-2s in standby storage at NAS North Island for possible future sales to France. France was using the F8F for ground attack in Indochina, a mission for which the United States Navy deemed the F8F unsuitable and was experiencing a high rate of attrition. However, events in Indochina changed before the remaining F8Fs were requested. By late 1957 or early 1958, these aircraft were deemed surplus and released for sale. Here begins their story.

*Opposite*: The F9F Panther replaced Bearcats on the Grumman production line and in the fleet. With the introduction of the Panther into fleet service in May 1949, Bearcats began to be withdrawn from front-line squadrons and sent to the reserves. The fourth production F9F-3, BuNo 122564, is shown during carrier acceptance trials aboard the USS *Franklin Roosevelt* (CV-42). (Aviation Photo Services Collection)

*Right*: F8F-1 BuNo 94956 was flown by the French and then was passed to the Royal Thai Air Force and is on display at the National Aviation Museum of the Royal Thai Air Force. (Dick Phillips Collection)

# Chapter 2

# IN SEARCH OF THE CIVIL CATS

Those 50 aircraft, placed in storage all those years ago, are the subject of this book. Of the 50, fewer than 35 survived into the 1960s, and the rest were "reclaimed" for parts for the South Vietnamese and Thai Bearcats, as were the very few remaining F8F-1s at Litchfield Park. Of this remaining handful, not all would survive or become civilian Cats.

When I first started research for this book, I was surprised to see so many civil-registered Bearcats. It wasn't until I started checking construction numbers (c/n), that I found that some civil Bearcats had as many as three civil registrations. Instead of 49 civil F8Fs, there were originally only 24. These 24 received US civil registration numbers ("N"), starting in 1958. Not all were from the NAS North Island group. One more was added to the civil rolls in 1978. Two more were registered in the 1990s, having been rescued from Southeast Asia. Another two are civil model G-58s (Grumman's design number for the F8F is 58), built as civil versions of the F8F. Neither received Bureau of Aeronautics Numbers (BuNo) serial numbers (s/n) or military equipment. This brings the total civil-registered Bearcat population to 29.

I included all known civilian registration numbers in the individual histories in an effort to track each aircraft's civilian history. However, to keep confusion to a minimum, this book will use the construction number (c/n[2]) as its guide. I have also made every effort to obtain accurate and factual information about each aircraft.

To tell the tale of the 29 civilian Cats, I talked to past and present owners as well as former service and civilian pilots. Each had a wonderful and varied experience with the Bearcat and I have included some of their stories. I interviewed people considered technically knowledgeable on F8Fs in both military and civil service, and obtained copies of all civilian accident reports in an effort to determine why, or if, the Bearcat is the killer that everyone claims. After reading these reports and talking with the pilots who have flown the F8F, I decided that part of this dialogue would be to dispel the legend of the killer "Cat."

## A Civilian Life Begins

After the F8F was withdrawn from military service, most were sent to Litchfield Park, AZ, or North Island, CA, for storage and eventual scrapping. Both facilities held mixed groups of F8F-1s and F8F-2s. The few that survived were either in foreign military service, held in reserve as replacement aircraft for those countries that were operating F8F, or to be reclaimed for parts. By 1958, those held in active storage (complete aircraft) for foreign countries were considered of no further use and were offered for sale. These F8Fs all had low airframe and engine hours. With a few exceptions, most had less than 1,000 airframe hours[3]. While one had only 460 hours total time (TT) when placed into storage, others had more. The prospect of obtaining a hot aircraft with low time was very attractive to many pilots. Plus, the aircraft could be had cheap. To obtain one meant outbidding the scrap man.

## The Dashes

At the time the F8Fs were offered for sale to the public, the only category open for registration was in the Limited Type Certificate (LTC) for the F8F-1[4]. A type certificate is issued by the United States Government Department of Commerce as its stamp of approval that a particular aircraft or engine meets all safety and airworthiness standards for the civil market.

---

2 All Grumman F8F c/ns begin with the letter D, for example, D.1081.

3 Airframe hours are the total number of hours an aircraft accumulates during flight operations, actual flying time since new. Engine hours total time are separate, as rarely does an airframe keep the same engine throughout its entire life and engines can be zero timed on rebuild/overhaul.

4 There are several levels of type certificates.

Grumman had obtained a LTC (LTC-23-2) in 1947 for its G-58A, a non-military F8F-1 company demonstrator flown by airshow/test pilot Al Williams. This was a real problem, since most of the aircraft for sale were F8F-2s for which there was no type certificate. The Limited Type Certificate was generally used to cover military aircraft converted to civil use or aircraft built in limited quantity for test and evaluation. Grumman had selected this route to register its G-58A instead of going for a complete and expensive Approved Type Certificate (ATC).

In 1958, the military had an agreement with the Federal Aviation Agency (FAA), that there would be no additional ex-military aircraft licensed in any category without a statement from the military that the aircraft had a satisfactory service life. This was due in part to the number of ex-military accidents. When the F8F-2s were submitted for registration under LTC-23-2 for the F8F-1s, the owners were informed by the FAA that there were enough differences in the Dash-1s and Dash-2s, such as taller tails and engines, that the Bearcats would have to be registered in a new category. This was not possible without a letter or statement from the United States Navy. However, if a letter could be obtained from the Navy, the FAA would license the F8F-2s in the Restricted Category.

Enter Roger Keeney of Acme Aircraft in Lomita, CA, and Roger Wolfe Kahn, Vice President of Grumman Aircraft. Acme Aircraft was an overhaul and repair facility that had experience in the overhaul and certification of ex-military aircraft in Southern California for several years. Keeney contacted Kahn and asked what could be done to solve the certificate problem. Keeney had someone with an F8F-2 who wanted to license it. Kahn was sympathetic to the cause, having flown the company-owned G-58B demonstrator for years. The G-58B was built at the end of F8F production, some claim from spare parts – a claim without facts. Kahn said he would see what he could do.

Short tail of the F8F-1 BuNo 95255. (Bob Kennedy)

*Above left*: Canopy and windscreen of the F8F-1, BuNo 95255. (Bob Kennedy)

*Above right*: Taller tail of the F8F-2 BuNo 122674. (Bob Kennedy)

*Left*: Canopy and windscreen of the F8F-2 BuNo 122674. (Bob Kennedy)

*Opposite*: P&W R-2800 engine installation in the *Chrome Cat* N2YY during restoration at the Aero-Sport facility in Chino, California, in February 1978. Note chromed landing gear and inner door covers, engine supports, and engine details. Much more chrome was added, such as the roll-over structure and tail-wheel mount. It was a "real shiny" ship. (Bob Kennedy)

FEDERAL AVIATION AGENCY

AR-32
Page 1
GRUMMAN
F8F-2

November 23, 1959

TYPE CERTIFICATE DATA SHEET NO. AR-32

This data sheet which is a part of type certificate No. AR-32 prescribes conditions and limitations under which the product for which the type certificate was issued meets the airworthiness requirements of the Civil Air Regulations.

Type Certificate Holder     Acme Aircraft Company
Lomita, California

I Model F8F-2 (Restricted Category), Approved November 2, 1959

| | |
|---|---|
| Engine | P&W R-2800-30W |
| Fuel | 115/145 or 100/130 Minimum grade aviation gasoline |
| Engine limits | Low - inter. - high impeller ratio. A.E.C. |
| | 7.29   9.15   10:55 |

| | HP | RPM | MP In.Hg. | Alt. |
|---|---|---|---|---|
| Maximum continuous | 1700 | 2600 | 44.0 | S.L. |
| 115/145 Fuel | 1800 | 2600 | 44.0 | 6000 |
| | 1450 | 2600 | 44.0 | 22000 |
| *Military Power | 2250 | 2800 | 60.0 | S.L. |
| *Military Power | 2090 | 2800 | 57.0 | 6000 |
| *Military Power | 1550 | 2800 | 56.0 | 22000 |
| Maximum continuous | - | 2600 | 44.0 | S.L. |
| 100/130 Fuel | - | 2600 | 44.0 | 6000 |
| | - | 2600 | 44.0 | 22600 |
| *Military Power | - | 2800 | 55.0 | S.L. |
| *Military Power | - | 2800 | 55.0 | 6000 |
| *Military Power | - | 2800 | 55.0 | 22000 |

*Takeoff Power

| | |
|---|---|
| Propeller | Aeroproducts Model No. A642-G4 |
| | Blade No. H20C1-162-11M5 or H20F-162-11M5 |
| Airspeed limits | Never exceed (Under 10,000 feet) 487 m.p.h. (425 knots) I.A.S. |
| | With Landing Gear extended      160 m.p.h. (140 knots) I.A.S. |
| | With Flaps extended       254 m.p.h. (220 knots) I.A.S. |
| | Reduce V_NE 2 knots/1000 feet above 10,000 feet |
| C.G. range | (+20.0) (19.26% M.A.C.) to (+25.9) (26.% M.A.C.) |
| Empty wt. C.G. range | None |
| Datum | Wing leading edge (35 in. outboard of fuselage sta. 68.57) |
| M.A.C. | 87.55 in. (L.E. M.A.C. +3.1 in. aft of datum) |
| Leveling means | Lugs inside fuselage at sta. 196 and 213 |
| Maximum weight | 10,200 lb. |
| No. of seats | 1 (+83.5) |
| Maximum baggage | None |

First page of the Federal Aviation Agency (FAA) Type Certificate AR-32 issued to Acme Aircraft Parts for the Grumman F8F-2 Bearcat, allowing it to be civil registered. See Chapter Six for complete document. (Aviation Photo Services Collection)

Shortly thereafter, Keeney received a copy of a letter from someone senior in the Navy stating that the F8F-2 Bearcats had a good service life[5]. Keeney took this to the local FAA office, finished the paperwork, and was issued a Restricted Category Type Certificate, number AR-32[6]. AR-32 was issued on November 23, 1959, to Acme Aircraft Co and "prescribed conditions and limitations under which the aircraft for which the type certificate was issued meets the airworthiness requirements to the Civil Air Regulations."

This type certificate covers only Grumman F8F-2s in the BuNo 121523–122708 serial block as being eligible for registration. These numbers were selected by the FAA. No explanation was given as to why the FAA made this selection. It should be noted, however, that all the surviving F8F-2s that were surplus fell within this range. Coincidence?

Any surplus Dash-1s would fall into the original LTC-23-2 Type Certificate issued in 1947. AR-32 further stated, "This airplane approved in restricted category for aerial photography only" and "There must be a placard/or marking prominently displayed in the cockpits in full view of the pilot," so stating.

I asked Roger Keeney why the type certificate stated for "aerial photography only." He told me that aerial photography was the easiest category to get approved. "All you had to do was reinstall the camera in the same location it was in while the plane was in military service and you had an aerial photo plane. You could tell the FAA you were going to take photos of your cattle and just fly over the field they were in and you met the requirement." A few F8F-1s did actually serve with aerial survey companies early in the 1960s. Other alterations typically carried out included[7]:

1. Removal of fuselage drop tank shackles and hardware.
2. Removal of armor plate.
3. Removal of catapult hooks.
4. Removal of armament switches and wiring.
5. Removal of gunsight computer system and harness.
6. Removal of all military radio equipment and controls.

---

5 It is rumored that Neil Armstrong, the first man on the moon, considered the F8F his favorite aircraft. He had flown them during his early naval flight training.

6 See Chapter Six for document.

7 See Chapter Six for other work carried out to meet requirements.

FORM ACA-500 (PART C) (3-56)

U. S. DEPARTMENT OF COMMERCE — CIVIL AERONAUTICS ADMINISTRATION

**BILL OF SALE**

84712

DOC. RECORDED 2 36 PM '58 CIVIL AERONAUTICS ADMINISTRATION OCT 2

For and in consideration of $611.99 the undersigned owner of the full legal and beneficial title of the aircraft described as follows:

AIRCRAFT MAKE AND MODEL
Grumman – Model F8F-2    N7826C

SERIAL NO.    REGISTRATION MARK
Bureau #121699

does this 15th day of August 19 58 hereby sell, grant, transfer, and deliver all of his right, title and interest in and to such aircraft unto:

(Name and address of purchaser—same as on Parts A and B of this form)

Acme Aircraft Parts, Inc.
P. O. Box 31
Compton, Calif.

and to his executors, administrators, and assigns, to have and to hold singularly the said aircraft forever, and certifies that same is not subject to any mortgage or other encumbrance except

| TYPE OF ENCUMBRANCE | AMOUNT | DATE |
| --- | --- | --- |
| None | | |
| IN FAVOR OF | | |

In testimony whereof ______ have set ______ hand and seal this ______ day of ______ 19 ___ U. S. Naval Air Station,

NAME OF SELLER North Island, San Diego 35, Calif.

BY (SIGN IN INK) J. C. ANNALORO
(If executed for co-ownership, all must sign)

TITLE Contracting Officer
(If signed for a corporation, partnership, owner, or agent)

ACKNOWLEDGMENT

State of California
County of San Diego 35

On this 18th day of August 1958 before me personally appeared the above named seller, to me known to be the person described in and who executed the foregoing bill of sale, and acknowledged that he executed the same as his free act and deed, and, if said bill of sale be that of a corporation swore that he was duly authorized to execute the same. Given under my hand and official seal the day and year written above.

NOTARY PUBLIC Charles E. Brasil
(SEAL)

MY COMMISSION EXPIRES August 12, 1960

FORWARD THIS COPY TO WASHINGTON — Retain Duplicate Copy.

Bill of Sale for F8F-2 BuNo 121699, c/n D.1073, from NAS North Island, California, to Acme Aircraft Parts on August 15, 1958, for $611.99. This was one of the lower prices paid for a Bearcat. The lowest price was $449.64 and the highest was $2,029.59. See Chapter Five for individual histories. (Aviation Photo Services Collection)

7. Remove boxes, brackets, and useless projecting parts in cockpit.

8. Install two new batteries and vents.

9. Install new radios and connections.

10. Reinstallation K-24 camera, in accordance with AR-32 specifications.

11. Re-cover all fabric surfaces.

The first F8F-2s that Keeney worked on were those owned by Ellis D. Weiner (known as E. D.), who would own or have access to five Bearcats. As they were brought in from storage (flown under a ferry permit), Keeney would put the aircraft into condition ready for licensing. He later worked on several others at his Torrance Municipal Airport facility where, during the early 1960s, F8Fs could always be found. Keeney purchased four directly.

Stinson Field Aircraft of San Antonio, Texas (TX), bought seven, four of which went to Transair Inc of Linden, New Jersey (NJ). Keeney's Acme Aircraft and Transair did most of the work to civilianize Bearcats. With the paperwork out of the way, 22 F8F-2s were put on the civil rolls.

Of these 22, two aircraft were bought by Stinson Field Aircraft from storage at NAS North Island. One, c/n D.1081, went directly to Kaman Helicopters, while the other, c/n D.1162, went to Transair and then to Kaman at its facility in Connecticut without being modified. Although civil registered, they were not flown again after their ferry flights to the Kaman facility. The aircraft were used as cross-wind generators for testing helicopters under various government contracts until 1970. These Bearcats were tied down next to the landing strip and run-up to produce crosswinds.

The first Dash-2 on the civil registry was c/n D.982, BuNo 121608. It was bought by E. D. Weiner on May 26, 1958, for $1,367.01 and registered N7700C. After Acme Aircraft did the conversion work, Weiner sold c/n D.982 to Grover Collins of Bakersfield, CA, on July 7, 1958, with a TT of 691.2 hrs. Collins only flew a total of 1.45hrs before selling it.

## Lonely Dash-1s

If the route F8F-2s took to the civil registry was arduous, the journey Dash-1s took was effortless. Grumman already held the Limited Type Certificate for F8F-1s, (LTC-23-2 issued August 29, 1947) to cover its company demonstrator, G-58A. This aircraft was a slightly modified F8F-1 with all of the military hardware removed, making it lighter and a better aerobatic performer. Any surplus F8F-1s could be licensed under this certificate. However, there weren't many Dash-1s around, as most had gone overseas under MDAP sales or had been reduced to spares or scrapped. By 1959, only two Dash-1s (XF8F-1, c/n D.18 and F8F-1, c/n D.628), plus the two G-58s (c/n D.739A, w/o 1949 and c/n D.1262) had been placed on the civil registry. C/n D.18 had come out of Litchfield Park in 1958 and c/n D.628 out of North Island in 1957. Twenty-four years later a third -1 was added. In 1978, an XF8F-1 c/n D.10 that had been in storage was registered. While records show there were some -1s still in storage, most were high-time airframes, making them less appealing to potential civilian owners.

The first Dash-1 on the civil registry was c/n D.628, BuNo 95356 that was sold from NAS North Island in November 1957 for $2,029.59 to Fred A. Kessler of Hollywood, CA, and registered as N7247C. Within days, Kessler sold it to E. D. Weiner, who immediately sold it to W. F. Patterson of Roselle, Illinois (IL), the same day.

## In from the Weather

Two Dash-1s were rescued from Southeast Asia. Dash-1 c/n D.779(a-1B) returned to the United States by way of France from Thailand in 1987. The second Dash-1, c/n D.527(a-1) also returned by way of France from Vietnam in 1990. Both had been on outside display as gate guardians in their respective countries since the 1960–70s. These two Bearcats were given United States civil registrations and are currently flying.

An F8F-1B c/n, D.804, BuNo 122120, was removed from its gate guardian position in Thailand and shipped to the United States in 1995. The F8F-1B was restored by retired Grumman employees for a Thai Air Force preservation group. It was shipped back to Thailand in early 2003, having not been flown or civil registered in the United States. Its first flight was in October 2005, and it does not carry a Thai civil registration.

F8F-1B, BuNo 122120, RTAF #1234 at Chiang Mai Air Base in Thailand prior to shipping to the United States for restoration by Grumman Aircraft in 1993. Following restoration, it was not registered or flown, but was shipped back to Thailand and flown in 2003. (Jim Dunn Collection)

# Chapter 3

# INTO CIVIL SERVICE

Some of the first items removed during civil conversion were all hardware for armament and stores, military radios and armor protection. Disconnection of the AEC on the Dash-2s could be done by bolting the throttle control linkage direct to the carburetor and bypassing the AEC. The *Navy Pilot's Handbook* (AN 01-85FD-1) states: "As a safety precaution, the AEC unit is so designed that in the event of failure of the unit's oil supply, the pilot will have manual control of the throttle below 45in at 2,800rpm." Some service pilots reported it was hard to keep the AEC adjusted. This also led to other problems trying to operate the P&W R-2800-30W without it. It is possible this action may have caused at least two early accidents.

Another later common modification was the removal of the R-2800-30W engines and replacing them with R-2800-CA16s engines, giving better performance and dependability. This change solved the problems associated with disconnecting the troublesome AEC. Other civil modifications were to the hydraulic systems, brakes, and fuel systems. Much of this work was based on fixes developed by the Navy shortly before the F8Fs were withdrawn from the fleet.

The R-2800-30W and the F8F-2 combination had its share of problems early in fleet service, as related by Pete Finley:

My introduction to the Bearcat occurred in June 1948, when I joined VF-61, part of Air Group 6 aboard the USS *Coral Sea* in Norfolk, Virginia (VA). We had brand new F8F-2s with P&W R-2800-30Ss. Having come from F6Fs in World War Two, this was a fighter pilot's dream. The F8F-2 made for a very pleasant year's cruise aboard Building 43, as the *Coral Sea* was affectionately known. While aboard the *Coral Sea* in 1949 our squadron, VF-61, suffered the loss of two F8F-2s following catapult launches.

Immediately thereafter all F8Fs in the Navy were grounded pending solution of the problem. Four of us in VF-61 more or less volunteered to take off from Oceana Naval Air Station, VA, climb to 10,000ft and fly a pattern between there and NAS Norfolk and back until we could get an engine to quit. We were all young, dedicated and sure that we could solve the problem.

We all did whiffer-drills, do-wah-ditties and 6 G pullouts for two days before Lt. Warren Rosser finally got his engine to quit. From 10,000ft, dead engine, he executed an approximate 270-degree left turn approach before he reached the seawall comprising the threshold of runway 18 at NAS Norfolk. His plane broke in half on the sea wall; the cockpit, Warren–unhurt–and the engine proceeding landward, with the tail feathers left plastered against the seawall.

The cause of the engine failures following catapult launch was found to be a fuel relief valve. This valve consisted of four cast aluminum body pieces surrounding a stainless-steel clamp. The wild torsional forces present during catapult launch and subsequent power reduction seized the valve in the fully relieved position; hence, no fuel pressure upon throttle reduction. As a postscript to this incident, we all learned that the F8F without power glides like a tool box.

This fact was yet to be appreciated by the F8Fs new civilian owners, especially those who chose to use the Bearcat for something other than aerial photography.

## Racing Bearcats

The Grumman F8F Bearcat was developed late in World War Two and remained in service into the early 1950s. When the National Air Races restarted in 1946 at Cleveland, Ohio (OH), there were no Bearcats available to race, unlike the many surplus P-51 Mustangs, Lockheed P-38s and Bell Cobras. While Navy F8Fs did appear and perform at Cleveland Races, none competed. The United States Navy's Flight Demonstration Team, the Blue Angels, performed with the F8F in 1946 and 1947. About the time Bearcats were surplus, the restarted post-war National Air Races at Cleveland ended.

The first race a Bearcat participated in was the initial National Championship Air Races at Reno, Nevada (NV), held in September 1964, when unlimited closed-course pylon air racing was revived. At the time, with its reputation for being a real hot ship, the Bearcat was a natural for this sport. Three F8F-2s lined up against five Mustangs for the beginning of the longest run of air racing at any one location. The Bearcats were c/n D.1020, Race #1, flown by Darryl Greenamyer; c/n D.1125, Race #80, flown by Mira Slovak; and c/n D.1126, Race #10, flown by Navy Commander Walt Ohlrich. The first race was won by Race #80, c/n D.1125, flown by Slovak on a race technicality, although he had placed second in the final race at 355.52mph. The late Bob Love in a P-51 Mustang had crossed the finish line first, but was penalized for cutting pylons. Greenamyer in Race #1, c/n D.1125, was disqualified for failing to land back at the racecourse. Ohlrich Race #10, c/n D.1126, took fifth in this historic event.

The last air race featuring a Bearcat was at Reno in 2015 when Race #77, c/n D.1171, flown by Stewart Dawson, placed second in the Gold Race at 471.957mph. (See Table 3).

Besides the Reno races, Bearcats have participated in races held at Mojave, CA, Miami, Florida (FL), Homestead, FL, Cape May, NJ, Lancaster, CA, Denver, Colorado (CO), San Diego, CA, Bakersfield, CA, Hamilton Air Force Base, CA, and Phoenix, AZ, with varying results[8]. Five Bearcats also participated in Transcontinental air racing[9] from 1967–71 with the best finish a second in 1970 by Gunther Balz in Race #9, c/n D.18, N9G.

During 51[10] years of racing, Grumman's Red Hot Cats have garnered Gold (first place) 23 times with the majority won by Lyle Shelton's hybrid Race #70/#77, c/n D.1171, N777L *Rare Bear*. Race #70/#77 won 16, 11 with Lyle Shelton at the helm and five under the pilotage of John Penny. The Bearcat with the most consecutive wins is Darryl Greenamyer's highly

---

8 See *Round-Engine Racers Bearcat & Corsairs* by Nicholas A. Veronico and A. Kevin Grantham

9 See *Wet Wings & Drop Tanks: Recollections of American Transcontinental Air Racing 1928–1970* by Birch Mathews

10 Total years; there were years when no Bearcats were raced

Bearcats competed when closed-course pylon racing returned in 1964. Bearcat Race #80, c/n D.1125, N9885C, was flown by Mira Slovak and chased by Mustang Race #8, N2869D. The Mustang was flown by Bob Love during the Championship race at Reno, Nevada, in 1964. (Emil Strasser)

One of the first three Bearcats to race in closed-course pylon racing was Race #1, c/n D.1020, N1111L, flown by Darryl Greenamyer. It competed at Reno, Nevada, during the inaugural race in 1964. It is shown after the 1964 Reno races. (Don Garrett via Jay Sherlock Collection)

modified Race #1, c/n D.1020, N1111L, with five at the Reno National Championship Air Races, 1965–69. After suffering landing-gear retraction problems during the 1970 Reno races, where he finished sixth, Greenamyer returned to win the 1971 races.

Darryl Greenamyer has six Gold wins, John Penny has five Gold wins (in #77), and Lyle Shelton has seven Golds at Reno. These records are unlikely to be broken by any other Bearcat pilot today. In addition to winning air races, both Bearcats, N1111L and N777L, hold world speed records for propeller-/piston-driven aircraft.

Race #10, c/n D.1126, also competed in the first race at Reno, Nevada, in 1964, flown by Walt Ohlrich. It is shown here in 1966 being raced by Sandy Falconer at Lancaster, California. The Bearcat also raced as #8 and #106. (Dusty Carter)

The third Bearcat to race at Reno, Nevada, in 1964 was Race #80, c/n D.1125, flown by Mira Slovak. He also raced it at Lancaster, California, in 1965 where this photo was taken. This Bearcat also raced as #41. (Dusty Carter)

*Left*: Three of the hottest fighters ever built are seen racing head-to-head at Lancaster, California, in 1965. Mira Slovak is in Bearcat #80, Dave Allender is in Mustang #19, and Darryl Greenamyer is in the P-38 #1. Greenamyer raced the P-38 while his #1 Bearcat was undergoing modification for Reno. (Emil Strasser)

*Opposite*: C/n D.1020, Race #1 at Lancaster, California, in 1966. Pilot Darryl Greenamyer had further modified D.1020 for racing. (Russ Hiatt)

Smirnoff
1
NIIIIL

C/n D.1261, Race #4, flown at Reno, Nevada, in 1974 by Jack Sliker. (William T. Larkins)

The third Bearcat to race at Reno, Nevada, in 1964 was Race #80, c/n D.1125, flown by Mira Slovak. He also raced it at Lancaster, California, in 1965 where this photo was taken. This Bearcat also raced as #41. (Dusty Carter)

*Left*: Three of the hottest fighters ever built are seen racing head-to-head at Lancaster, California, in 1965. Mira Slovak is in Bearcat #80, Dave Allender is in Mustang #19, and Darryl Greenamyer is in the P-38 #1. Greenamyer raced the P-38 while his #1 Bearcat was undergoing modification for Reno. (Emil Strasser)

*Opposite*: C/n D.1020, Race #1 at Lancaster, California, in 1966. Pilot Darryl Greenamyer had further modified D.1020 for racing. (Russ Hiatt)

C/n D.1261, Race #4, flown at Reno, Nevada, in 1974 by Jack Sliker. (William T. Larkins)

C/n D.18, Race #7 at Reno, Nevada, in 1969 flown by Gunther Balz, who had also competed in the 1969 Transcontinental Race. (William T. Larkins)

C/n D.1122, Race #7, flown by Butch Morris at the 1971 Mojave, California, races. This Bearcat had been entered at Reno in 1966, but did not qualify. (Dick Phillips Collection)

C/n D.1126, Race #8, being raced by John Herlihy at Reno, Nevada, in 1973. The aircraft also competed as #10 and #106. (William T. Larkins)

C/n D.1126, Race #8, flown by Bill Whittington in 1981 at Reno, Nevada. Race #8 was also flown by Don Whittington at Homestead, Florida, in 1979. This Bearcat also races as #10 and #106. (William T. Larkins)

C/n D.1181, Race #11, taxiing out for the start of a race at Reno, Nevada, in 1966. Flown by Chuck Klusmann for owner John Church. Klusmann would place fourth in the Consolation race. Race #11 also raced as #24 and #99. (Emil Strasser)

*Left*: C/n D.10, Race #14, flown by Howard Pardue who competed at Reno, Nevada, from 1984–2009 and at seven other racing events. (Jim Dunn)

*Opposite*: C/n D.1148, Race #23, competed only once, in 2007, at Reno, Nevada, flown by Dave Morss. (Jerry Liang)

14
23
P
Provenance
FIGHTER SALES
NAVY
DENVER
NX14WB
F8F-2
NAVY
122619
14

*Above*: C/n D.1181, Race #24, at the 1973 Reno Air Races in Nevada, flown by its owner Bud Fountain. Number 24 also raced as #11 and #99. (William T. Larkins)

*Opposite*: C/n D.1125, Race #41, raced at both Mojave, California, where this photo was taken, and Reno, Nevada, in 1973. Number 41 was flown by Mike Smith. It also raced as #80. (Russ Hiatt)

417
Lois Jean
41
121751

*Above*: C/n D.1105, Race #44, was flown by Ron Reynolds at Reno, Nevada, in 1970. It also completed in the 1970 Transcontinental Race and in San Diego, California, in 1971. It also raced as #66. (William T. Larkins)

*Opposite*: C/n D.1162, Race #52, was entered in the 2011 Reno Air Races in Nevada by Nelson Ezell, but it did not qualify. (Mike Henniger)

Blue Angels
Bella
52
U.S.NAVY
1
GRUMMAN BEARCAT

C/n D.1105, Race #66, at Mojave, California, where it competed in the 1970 California 1000 Mile Race. (Jerry Liang)

C/n D.1171, Race #70, at its first race in 1969 at Reno, Nevada. It was flown by Lyle Shelton. It also raced as #77. (William T. Larkins)

C/n D.1171, Race #77, at the 1971 Cape May, New Jersey, races flown by Lyle Shelton. It also raced as #70. (Dick Phillips Collection)

C/n D.1171, Race #77, taxiing out for a test run at the 1976 Mojave, California, races. See caption below for the results. It also raced as #70. (Bob Kennedy)

C/n D.1171, Race #77, after engine failure at Mojave, California, in 1976. There was no serious damage. (Aviation Photo Services Collection)

C/n D.1171, Race #77, showing the aftermath of the Mojave 1976 slide. This put #77 out of racing for a number of years. (Bob Kennedy)

C/n D.1190, Race #98, competed at both the Mojave, California, and Reno, Nevada races, piloted by John Church and John Herlihy. Shown at Reno in 1972 and flown by Church. (William T. Larkins)

C/n D.902, Race #99, during its only Reno, Nevada, appearance in 1968. It was flown in the earlier Transcontinental race by its owner Bob Kucera. (Ron Olsen)

C/n 1126, Race #106, was flown by William Anders at the 1998 and 1999 Reno Air Races in Nevada. It also raced as #8 and #10. (Russ Hiatt)

C/n D.527, Race #204, flown by Alan Preston at Reno, Nevada, 1997–99. It is one of three F8F-1s to race. (Bob Kennedy)

C/n D.1122, Race #224, at Reno, NV, in 2007, flown by Ray Dieckman. In the background are #14 and #23. Bearcat #77 is not shown. Four Bearcats raced in 2007. (Jerry Liang)

## Speed Records

There was once a quest to be the first pilot to set the record for flying faster than 100 miles per hour. Since that record was set, pilots have pursued the goal of advancing this achievement. Of the world speed records, none is more prestigious than the 3 kilometer (km) record for Class C, Group 1 (powered by piston engines) aircraft. The rules in use when Bearcats set their records were complex. An aircraft must fly a 3km course that has been constructed to rigid National Aeronautics Association (NAA) standards. The course measures a total of 5km end-to-end with times taken over the center 3km. The pilot cannot go above 150 meters on the course or above 500 meters on the end turn arounds. In a 30-minute period, the pilot can make unlimited passes over the course; however, the record

The start of Heat-3 at the 1965 Reno Air Races in Nevada, showing from far left # 80 Mira Slovak, #1 Darryl Greenamyer, #21 Bob Abrams in the red Mustang, and Bob Hoover in the yellow pace plane about ready to release everyone. (Emil Strasser)

is based on the four fastest consecutive passes. Ground spotters are located at each end of the 5km markers, while high-speed cameras are stationed at each end of the 3km course. Spotter aircraft maintain coverage of the course at both ends and the middle to verify the aircraft does not exceed the allowable altitude during the run. All records are considered unofficial until verified by the NAA. Once verified as a record, the information is sent to the Federation Aeronautique Internationale (FAI) for certification of a new world record.

On September 12, 1929, a Supermarine S-6 set the record at 357.7mph. Ten years later, on April 26, 1939, a Messerschmitt Bf-109R boosted the record to 469.220mph. The record stood for 30 years. Enter Darryl Greenamyer and Bearcat c/n D.1020, N1111L. Flying over a course set out over Edwards Air Force Base in the California Mojave Desert, Greenamyer and his aircraft set a new world record of 482.462mph[11] on August 16, 1969. Greenamyer had tried twice before for the record. In 1966, he had to abort his attempt due to lateral instability after shortening the tail by 18in, and again in 1968 after burning a piston.

Greenamyer's Bearcat c/n D.1020 had been extensively modified with a cut-down F-1-style bubble canopy, clipped wings (clipped by 7ft), a 13ft, 6in AD-6 Skyraider prop, P-51H prop spinner, a water boil-off oil-cooling system, which allowed covering the wing air intakes, and smoothing out the wing leading edge. The aircraft's P&W R-2800-30W engine was tuned to produce 3,300hp. The story goes that c/n D.1020 ran so hot that Greenamyer had to wear mukluks on his feet and an insulated glove on his throttle hand to keep them from blistering, something that had happened during previous attempts.

Records are made to be broken and the 3km was no exception; almost 20 years to the day, Greenamyer brought the record to the United States. Lyle Shelton and his hybrid c/n D.1171, N777L, shattered it on August 21, 1989. The Bearcat featured clipped wings (clipped by 5ft), cut-down canopy and a massive Wright R-3350 3,000hp engine. Flying over a course set up in Las Vegas, New Mexico (NM), Shelton and c/n D.1171 set a new world record of 528.329mph.[12] One unofficial pass was timed at 541mph; not bad for a 40-year-old aircraft.

Another record held by the F8F is the time-to-climb record for propeller-/piston-engine aircraft to 10,000ft (3,000m), first set by an F8F-1 in 1946 in 94 seconds. In August 1951, at the National Air Races held in Detroit, Michigan (MI), the United States Navy conducted a climb contest between an F8F and a McDonnell F2H-1 Banshee jet fighter. From a standing start, the Bearcat beat the Banshee to 10,000ft in slightly less than one and one-half minutes. This record remained until broken by Lyle Shelton and c/n D.1171 on February 6, 1972, when it took only 91.9 seconds to reach 10,000ft (3,000m) at Thermal. CA. Lyle Shelton, c/n D.1171, and his team achieved an impressive record with these two records and 16 Gold race wins, more than any other F8F.

## The Dark Side of Racing

While air racing has produced two well-known Bearcat champions, racing has also produced its share of Bearcat fatalities. There have been four Bearcat accidents attributed to air racing, two of which occurred during races. The first racing fatality happened during the 1971 United States Cup Race in San Diego, CA, and involved c/n D.1105, N5005.

### July 17, 1971

Ron Reynolds was the pilot of c/n D.1105, N5005 when the Bearcat first appeared at the 1970 Reno National Championship Air Races (NCAR). The aircraft carried Race #44 at Reno and placed second in the Silver race. Reynolds had dropped out of the Transcontinental Race at Sioux City, Iowa (IA), with engine problems before the Reno Air Races. Later in the year, at Mojave for the California 1000 Race, the Bearcat carried Race #66 and placed 18th after dropping out on lap 17 with a burned piston.

In 1971 c/n D.1105, again as Race #44, was entered in the United States Cup Race held in San Diego, on July 16–17. This was a 1,000-mile race like Mojave. The ten-mile racecourse was laid out over the old Naval Auxiliary Air Station at Brown Field and consisted of eight pylons, with pilots flying in a clockwise pattern. There were 13 aircraft entered, with Lyle Shelton in Race #77, c/n D.1171, the fastest qualifier at 324.3mph.

Ron Reynolds started in Race #44, with co-owner Mike Geren taking over about midway for the race on Sunday, July 17. Reynolds took off in the second group of the staggered start. By the end of lap 9, #44 was fifth behind Shelton with Mustangs in first through third. Reynolds came in on lap 17 for the first of his pit stops and then made his

---

11  The elusive 500mph mark would have to wait. Steve Hinton in the *Red Baron* RB-51 Mustang came close in August 1979 with a record of 499.018mph

12  A new record of 531.34mph was set in September 2017 by Steven Hinton in the P-51 Voodoo. Shelton's record still stands as the FIA made a slight change to the 3km rules

second stop on lap 45. By lap 60, #44 was in sixth place with Mike Geren having relieved Reynolds during a previous pit stop. As #44 came around to complete lap 76, smoke was seen pouring from the right side of the engine. Geren pulled up and climbed to good altitude (about 500ft) north of the airport, with fire now clearly visible. He was turning to set up for landing the burning Bearcat when it suddenly nosed over, fell into a field at a steep angle, and exploded in a massive fireball.

The Federal Aviation Administration (FAA) investigated the crash of Race #44, c/n D.1105. Robert Griscom, who was at the races along with nine other FAA inspectors, was one of the accident investigators, and also wrote the final report. In 1984, Mr Griscom sent me the following letter.

As you may know, the NTSB reserves the right to determine "probable cause" on the basis of reports prepared in the field, so I will not attempt to do that. I can give you the facts as I recall them, and you can draw your own conclusions. The accident started with an engine failure when the rear cylinder at the 5 o'clock position separated from the power section. This caused a fire which emerged from the cowling's lower right side, almost directly in front of the cockpit air intake at the wing root. This oil-fed fire eventually did flow back along the fuselage to the empennage and burned the fabric control surfaces prior to impact. The pilot was wearing a parachute, but did not attempt to exit the aircraft. He had an oxygen mask available, but was not wearing it.

It is interesting to note that each of the ten FAA inspectors who witnessed the accident had a different picture of the series of events. Fortunately for the record, ABC Sports was filming the event, and we were able to study this film. The film showed the engine fire initially as the aircraft made its turn from the main straightaway at about 20–30ft above ground level [AGL]. The aircraft then pulled up to about 500ft on a downwind leg, paralleling Runway 26L. It was during this period the fire spread back along the fuselage. The aircraft then turned toward the runway and pitched down. The film showed the landing gear extending, then immediately retracting again–at about this time, the elevator fabric was seen to burn. The aircraft crashed in about a 15-degree nose-down attitude, ¼ mile north of runway 26L. The engine separated on impact, and the aircraft burned. Attempts by Crash and Rescue personnel to rescue the pilot were not successful. The pilot appeared to be trying to save the aircraft not realizing how serious the fire was.

The NTSB report, LAX72FUM03, contained the remarks under probable cause, "material failure–internal engine failure during air race. Engine and aircraft caught fire. Abnormal power settings were used." Mike Geren was 32 years old, with 4,359 total hours and 38 hours in type. On its last FAA inspection report of June 4, 1971, c/n D.1105 had 986.5 hours total time.

## October 21, 1973

The next racing tragedy involved c/n D.1181, N148F, and took place during the 1973 Mojave California National Air Races. This Bearcat began its racing career at the 1966 National Champion Air Races (NCAR) at Reno as Race #11 while owned by John Church, one of three that he would own. Race #11 was flown by Chuck Klusmann, who placed the overall red Bearcat fourth in the Consolation Race. Church raced the fairly stock c/n D.1181 at Reno in 1967, where it placed second in the Consolation Race. In 1968, Church sold the now black and gold c/n D.1181 to Hawke Flying Service, owned by Walter "Bud" Fountain Jr., on November 1, 1968. Bearcat c/n D.1181 next appeared at Reno in 1969 with a bare metal fuselage and black tail and was flown by Fountain as Race #99. However, engine and mechanical problems kept c/n D.1181 from qualifying for the 1969 races.

By 1973, c/n D.1181 was ready to return to air racing, now with a bare metal fuselage and red tail. Fountain had replaced the original R-2800-30W engine with an R-2800-CB16[13] engine and added a -44 nose case, so he could use a Skyraider prop. Fountain also completed a general clean-up of the airframe, and the aircraft carried Race #24. Fountain qualified tenth at Reno at 378.9mph and placed second in a Heat Race. During the Unlimited Championship Race on Sunday, September 16, Race #24 developed problems. These were reported to be a broken hydraulic line, possibly caused by severe vibrations due to the engine and gear case combination, and Race #24 dropped out on lap 5.

Just over a month later, c/n D.1181 was racing in the California Air Classic at Mojave, CA. These races were held from October 18–21, 1973, at the former MCAS Mojave over an eight-mile oval course. Fountain qualified fourth fastest at 363.2mph on Friday, October 19, assuring a slot in the Unlimited Gold Race on Sunday.

---

13  The -CB16 was considered a transport engine. It was used on the DC-6 and other airliners and had a more dependable reputation

It was during qualifying that c/n D.1181 again developed a problem, necessitating Fountain and his crew to work through the night to make repairs in order for #24 to race the next day. It has been rumored and speculated for years that Fountain did not race on Saturday, October 20, because of what he found while repairing c/n D.1181 on Friday night.

On the Sunday, Fountain made the decision to race in Heat-1A. The contestants for the six-lap race were: #33 Ken Burnstine in a P-51 Mustang, #5 Jack Sliker in a Mustang, #9 John Crocker, also in a Mustang, #38 Gary Levitz in his P-38 Lightning, and #24 Bud Fountain in c/n D.1181. The race was fairly uneventful, as the only real battle was between Burnstine and Sliker for first. Levitz and Crocker both dropped out toward the end of the race with mechanical problems. Burnstine won the race with a speed of 367.6mph, followed by Sliker in second and Fountain in third. As the race ended, Fountain appeared to pull up to gain altitude prior to landing after passing pylon 1. At approximately 250ft, a mass of flame and smoke could be seen pouring from the obviously mortally wounded Bearcat. Suddenly c/n D.1181 pitched over and impacted into the desert at about a 70-degree angle. The resulting fire consumed the shattered remains. I remember watching dense black smoke billowing up and hoping that maybe Fountain had survived. The death of Bud Fountain and loss of c/n D.1181 was the first aircraft accident I witnessed, and would not be the last. Due to the fragmented nature of the remains the accident report (NTSB LAX74FUQ16) stated, "a possible rear engine case failure which caused a fire in the engine compartment that spread into the cockpit area." It is reported that during the process to lighten #24, the stainless-steel heat bulkhead between the engine compartment and the oil tank had been removed.[14]

An eerie side note to Heat-1A; with the death of Gary Levitz at the 1999 Reno Air Races, all the participants of Heat-1A at the 1973 Mojave race died in aircraft crashes.

**December 12, 1968**
The other two possible racing-related Bearcat accidents happened after both Bearcats were away from the racecourse. The first befell c/n D.902, N212KA, an F8F-2 that had been modified for aerial survey work with the installation of a second seat and window in the aft fuselage.

Race #99, c/n D.902, N212KA, only competed twice, both times by its owner Robert "Bob" Kucera during the 1968 racing season. The tragedy may have started for c/n D.902 during the 1968 Harold's Club Transcontinental Trophy Race, which was an attempt at reviving the Bendix Transcontinental Race of the 1930s and 1940s.

The late aviation historian Dusty Carter related the following story about c/n D.902 Race #99 to me in a letter dated March 16, 1983.

Bob Kucera and seven other Unlimited pilots took off in the early morning hours of September 15, 1968, from the Milwaukee Municipal Airport to begin the Harold's Club Transcontinental Trophy Race. [Author's note: Harold's Club was a well-known casino in downtown Reno.] The speed dash across the United States was reminiscent of the famous Bendix races of the Golden Age of air racing. The 1968 race would cover a distance of 1,667 miles from Milwaukee to Reno with contestants allowed to make refueling stops along the way. The winner was judged to be the first aircraft arriving at the Reno/Stead airport with the fastest time. For the transcontinental race N212KA had been fitted with long-range drop tanks, (it already had wet wings, a modification added when it had been converted for aerial photography), which would give sufficient range to fly the race without stopping. Within an hour or so, Kucera was forced to put N212KA down in Kansas due to a very rough and hot running engine. The cause was found to be a lack of sufficient oil in the engine. The oil was nearly gone when he landed, but he could find no leaks or other problems. [Author's note: Some sources report there was metal in the oil screen, a sure sign that his engine had suffered damage.]

Upon refilling the oil tank, Kucera again headed for Reno where he finished fourth in the transcon race. At Reno he suffered no other problems. He placed first in the Unlimited Consolation Race at 331.8mph on September 21. The oil loss during the transcon remained a mystery. After the race, Kucera flew N212KA home to Ohio.

N212KA crashed on December 12, 1968, at Lost Nation Airport Willoughby, Ohio. I understand the cause of the crash was engine failure just after take-off. Engine failure due to the failure of the hydraulic damper on the crankshaft causing breakage of the connecting rods on the rear bank of cylinders. Kucera died in the local hospital shortly thereafter. The oil loss could have been the beginning of the problem.

Robert Kucera was 46 years old, with 12,250 hours total time. The NTSB report (CHI69FO620) states probable cause as: "Engine failure–master and connecting rods–counterweight rollers p/n.91870 backed out of counterweight and sheared all rods–collided with trees." Bearcat c/n D.902 had around 1,400 hours TT.

Dusty's letter continued on the subject of the next off-racecourse accident involving Bearcat c/n D.1261, N7701C, the last production-built F8F.

---

14  Note this may also be the case with the crash of c/n D.1105.

C/n D.1020, N1111L after it set a new world speed record of 482.462mph in August 1969. It was flown by Darryl Greenamyer at the Reno Air Races in September 1970. (Jerry Liang)

**September 1975**

After several years of racing P-51s John "Jack" Sliker acquired F8F-2, N7701C, Race #4 and modified it for racing. His first race was at Miami in 1973. He qualified first and placed second in the Championship Race. Sliker had replaced the stock P&W R-2800 engine with an R-2800-CB-17 from a Martin 404 airliner, resulting in a large ram air inlet ahead of the windshield to accommodate the downdraft carburetor system used on the 404. Other changes included removal of military equipment and stripping the Bearcat down to bare metal and clipping the wings. In 1974, #4 qualified sixth at Reno at 396mph, but developed engine problems during Heat-1B and did not finish. However, for the Unlimited Medallion Race #4

C/n D.902, N212KA receiving attention on the ramp during the 1968 Reno Air Races after finishing fourth in the Transcontinental race. The cause of its oil loss during that race was never solved. (Jerry Liang)

placed first, which bumped N7701C into the Consolation Race. The race was mildly exciting with Sliker in #4 battling with Howie Keefe in #11 *Miss America*. Keefe and his Mustang prevailed and Sliker and #4 took second. Later, in October, Sliker was able to push N7701C to fifth fastest qualifier at the California National Air Races at Mojave. During the Championship Race Sliker again finished behind *Miss America* to place fourth.

For 1975, N7701C qualified fifth at 397mph at the California National Air Races held at Mojave during June. N7701C won the Unlimited Silver Race at 374mph and finished fourth in the Championship Race. The 1975 Reno races that September saw #4 again a fast qualifier at 393.3mph, which was the eighth fastest, and again #4 took first in the Silver. The Bearcat would race as a fill-in for the injured N1111L with landing gear trouble, in the Championship Race and was able to place third in one of the wildest Reno finishes.

The 1975 Reno was the last race for #4. On the return flight to Wadley, Georgia (GA), Sliker's home town, N7701C suffered engine stoppage on approach to the Flagstaff, AZ, runway, resulting in a fatal crash.

In a letter written by well-known F8F pilot and owner Harold "Bubba" Beal[15] to *Air Classics* magazine in March 1979, he put forth the following theory as to the cause of c/n D.1261, N7701C's demise.

Jack Sliker was a good pilot but he used poor judgement. His fuel gauge was inoperative at the Reno Air Races and he did not wear his oxygen mask when he left, [just] as Bud Fountain did not wear his at Mojave. If you do not seal the cockpit air intake, which travels through the accessory section, then you are going to get carbon monoxide poisoning if you do not use oxygen. All of the old fighters have had drop tank cables and armament wiring removed that traveled through the firewalls and people do not seal them back up. I personally observed such inadequate air ducts in Mike Geren's, Bud Fountain's and Jack Sliker's airplanes. Jack had carbon monoxide poisoning and tried to make too long a cross-country flight on too small [little] fuel. The Bearcat does not glide like a brick, it glides very well like a P-51 does, but when you put the gear down you must have enough altitude to compensate for the drag and increased rate of descent. With carbon monoxide in his system Jack probably did not care if he made it or not.

Sliker's c/n D.1261, N7701C, impacted a small hill just short of the runway threshold, out of gas. The NTSB report (LAX76FUJ23) listed the probable cause as: "Inadequate preflight preparation and/or planning – mismanagement of fuel–fuel exhaustion–miscalculated fuel consumption. Other–complete power loss–aircraft struck embankment 100ft from runway 21 approach end." Jack Sliker was 49 years old and had 23,000 hours TT.

## Spar Caps and Tweaked Wings

Several changes to stock Bearcats are said to contribute to the controversy that has led to the Bearcat's notoriety as a dangerous aircraft. These are spar caps and tweaked wings.

Dear Mr Kennedy,

In your quest to track down the civil histories of the remaining F8Fs, I thought you may be interested in the military background of two of these aircraft, BuNos 121589 (c/n D.963) and 121679 (c/n D.1053). I flew both of these airplanes in 1951/52 as a member of AES-12 (Aircraft Engineering Squadron Twelve) at MCAS Quantico, VA. We were the US Marine Corps Close Air Support Demonstration Squadron and the only Marine squadron to fly the F8F. [Author's note: VMT-1 at MCAS Cherry Point, NC, and VMFT-20 also at Cherry Point were the two squadrons assigned to AES-12. MTG-20 at MCAS El Toro, CA, had VMT-2 and VMFT-10 with F8Fs.] In October 1951 one of the F8F-2s lost a wing recovering from a practice dive-bombing run [Author's note: BuNo 121670.] Subsequent inspections by Bureau of Aeronautics United States Navy (BuAer) engineers revealed each of our 24 a/c made a least 200 practice dive-bombing/rocket runs per month and exceeded 9Gs at least once each flying day. Two a/c inspected by O&R at NAS Oceana revealed each had cracks in the main wing spar. They just couldn't take the punishment we were giving them. We retired them from our squadrons service on June 5, 1952. The F8F was the most thrilling, thoroughly exhilarating airplane I have ever flown.

Thomas E. Archer, Major USMC (Ret.),
May 17, 1984

In response to this problem, Bureau of Aeronautics United States Navy (BuAer) issued *F8F AIRCRAFT SERVICE CHANGE No. 137* on May 1954 that stated:

*Subject: Wing: reinforcement of center section*
This led to one of the most controversial changes to the F8F. To increase the strength of the center section of the wing BuAer ordered the installation of three reinforcement bars in the

---

15  Harold Beal owned or co-owned five F8Fs over the years

lower cap strip of the main beam wing center section. These bars were between the port and starboard landing gear ribs and on the lower surface of the wing.

To install these bars, it would be necessary to drill holes through the main wing spar, (see Chapter Six for complete AD), a procedure Grumman advised against. Grumman felt this would degrade the integrity of the spar and shorten the useful life of the aircraft. However, by 1954 the Navy was already withdrawing the F8F from service, so aircraft lifespan was not of importance. It was important that those F8Fs remaining in service with training and utility units remained safe to fly. It should be remembered that the Navy was not interested in the F8F having a life after it had been withdrawn from service, nor a civil life.

It does make one to wonder how many French and Thai aircraft had wing failures since they were using Bearcats as ground-support aircraft. Would this modification have helped prevent failures or increase them?

While this act may not have had an effect on the Bearcats remaining in naval service, it does perhaps have an effect on their civil life.

The late well-known warbird pilot/restorer Elmer Ward said: "Spar cap reinforcement– this is a classic Bearcat subject. The stated reason for this is to 'increase the strength of the center section of the wing and extend the useful life of the wings for repeated application of high loads.'"

This is not the end of the story. During a long phone discussion with Corkey Fornof, the son of Bill, he told a different tale. Fornof said he investigated the spar cap question extensively after his father's wing separated in flight, c/n D.982, N7700C. His version is that the strap was a Navy modification that was undertaken when the Marine Corps started operating the Bearcat as a dive bomber at a weight limit of 15,000lb. They found that under some conditions, they were experiencing rivet failure and consequent spar distortion at these loads. The Navy came up with the modification and applied it only to those aircraft used by the Marine Corps for the dive-bombing mission. [Author's note: You will probably note that this does not co-ordinate with the application of which aircraft the Service Bulletin applies to.]

He further claims that Grumman did not sanction the modification and was of the opinion that it may do more harm than good. This sounds plausible because it puts a number of big holes throughout the spars. Grumman points out that it did not incorporate the modification in the aircraft made for the vice president of the company, c/n D.1262, N700A, even though it could easily have been accomplished on the line.

Neither Fornof aircraft had the modification and Lyle Shelton removed the spar caps from his hybrid racer. "I don't plan to put them on mine, c/n 1081, N3035," Elmer Ward said on February 6, 1984, during the rebuilding project.

During a phone conversation I had with John Dowd, he related that he had decided not to put them on the two F8Fs he was rebuilding, believing, like Grumman, that putting large holes through the spar can't be healthy.

Lyle Shelton, c/n D.1171, N777L, and Darryl Greenamyer, c/n D.1020, N1111L, both removed the spar caps from their Bearcats due to their racers not needing them. When they clipped the wings for racing, this effectively negated the need as the clipped wings removed some of the flex and reduced the loading on the wings.

This is what Grumman originally tried to accomplish by giving the F8Fs jettisonable wing tips. The theory was, as the Japanese Kamikazes were making their death plunge toward our ships, the Bearcat would be fast enough to overtake them and shoot them out of the air. Remember Grumman built them as lightweight interceptors, not as air-to-air fighters like the Hellcat. One problem was the tremendous speed built up by the Bearcat in the chase. Upon pulling out of their dive, the Bearcats could shed their wings. Grumman's fix was to install safety wing tips that under high-wing loading, such as a high-speed pull-up, the outer 3ft of each wing tip would jettison. Each wing had an explosive prima cord detonator, thus reducing the loading and allowing a safe recovery.

After several uncommanded breakaways, some resulting in asymmetrical configurations, and the loss of at least one aircraft, the Navy and Grumman eliminated the jettisonable tips and its associated prima cord device and limited the Bearcat to 4Gs in 1949. (See Chapter Six.) It is rumored that one aircraft maintainer was killed by an accidental discharge of a wing tip.

Enter the Marine Corps in 1951, with its need for a close-air support trainer, and the F8F was handy because the fleet was withdrawing them from front-line service. As Major Archer stated in his letter, they lost an aircraft during a close-air support pull out. To fix the problem, the Navy installed spar caps to strengthen the wing.

Well-known warbird restorer and pilot Steve Hinton has called the spar-cap modification a "band-aid" and did not plan to install them on the Bearcat he was restoring, c/n D.739A, N3025. He feels there is no need for them under standard civil operation. Hinton holds perhaps the largest number of flight hours for a Bearcat pilot today, with time in more than six different F8Fs. He further states, without a doubt, the Bearcat is his favorite aircraft.

C/n D.1261, N7701C rounding a pylon at the 1975 Reno Air Races where Jack Sliker would finish third in the Championship race. Unfortunately, he was fatally injured on his way home from the Reno races. (Jay Miller Collection)

C/n D.628 undergoing restoration in Texas. Compare this photo with photo on page 112 showing what the Bearcat looked like before restoration. (Jay Miller)

C/n D.628 before having its engine hung and showing all the necessary plumbing and ducting. (Jay Miller)

C/n D.628 after installation of a P&W R-2800 engine, landing gear, and windscreen. Note how the engine exhaust is piped. The restoration work on N4752Y is top notch. (Jay Miller)

I would like to point out that in over 60 years of civil operation there has been only one civil F8F crash, c/n D.982, N7700C, caused by a wing failure, and it was an un-capped wing. I believe the spar-cap issue is one of those cases where people are looking for causes and this issue has not contributed to any accidents in the Bearcat's civil life.

While spar caps may not be an issue in safe civil Bearcat operation, the subject of the tweaked wing is. This flight characteristic is caused by someone having the aircraft jacked or towed with the fuel-bay door removed, with the engine still attached. This door is an integral part of the structure. It is not hinged like a door, but is more of a panel held in place by bolts. When taking off in a tweaked F8F, as soon as the gear is up and locked, the aircraft exceeds 200Kt with zero trim setting in three axis; the aircraft yaws right and rolls right.

The trim will override this tendency, but increased speed increases the problem. Rerigging the flight controls will not help. The right wing has been permanently tweaked due to removal of the stress door and moving or jacking the aircraft.

Some pilots like Lyle Shelton, Howard Pardue and Harold Beal felt this was a greater problem than the spare cap issue, especially for pilots not knowing their aircraft are so affected. The only fix is a new wing assembly. While there have been no known documented accidents in civil F8Fs due to this problem, some have felt there is the potential.

Factory photo of BuNo 94802 showing that a Bearcat could be brought back safely with only one wing tip. After a fatal accident in December 1945, the Navy and Grumman conducted numerous tests to fix the problem of uncommanded wing-tip separations. Though several fixes were tried, the jettisonable wing tips were finally abandoned in 1949. (Grumman Corp.)

Cn. D.1262, N700A and c/n D.982, N7700C on the ramp in St. Louis, Missouri, before an airshow in 1970. The Bearcats were flown by father and son, Bill and Corkey Fornof. (Jay Miller Collection)

C/n D.1088 N700H, #100, and c/n D.1126 N800H while owned by B&S Advertising (Bubba Beal and Chub Smith). (Harold Beal)

C/n D.1088, N700H, #100, and c/n D.1125, N9885C, #200, at an airshow in August 1979. Beal and Smith would own a total of five Bearcats before the death of Smith in c/n D.1125. (Harold Beal)

# Chapter 4

# IS THE CAT A KILLER?

Grumman's "Red Hot Cat" has long held a reputation for being a killer, or at least, very difficult to fly. Flying any type of high-performance aircraft is dangerous, whether current military or ex-military. Even the simplest of aircraft can be difficult or deadly to operate. Multiple factors enter into the safe operation of any aircraft including weather, mechanical soundness and human factors. Perhaps the most unpredictable and deadliest is the human factor. When examining civil Bearcat accident reports, I believe the human factor is the leading cause of an accident.

Bearcat accident statistics reveal 17 major F8F accidents have befallen the civil Cats. Of the 28 flyable civil-registered Cats, nine have been written off in fatal accidents. Eight have been in non-fatal accidents where the aircraft sustained major damage. Two of the eight each sustained two major accidents during their civil lives (c/n D.10 and c/n D.1171). Three have had minor accidents.

By comparison, the 74 known civil-registered Lockheed P-38s have had 15 write-offs and 11 non-fatal write-offs. The North American P-51 has even higher percentages. From 1960 to 2023, 64 Mustangs were written off and 38 heavily damaged.

I believe human error is the cause of these accidents after reviewing and analyzing the accident reports[16].

Mustang N6174C was sold as surplus in September 1957 for $801.11. In March 1958, it was written off after the pilot lost control on take-off, illustrating the hazards of operating high-performance aircraft. (Dick Phillips Collection)

---

16 In listing the civil accidents, I have excluded the four racing accidents already covered

P-38L N5596V at Winslow, Arizona, in August 1992 after mechanical issues caused the pilot to make a gear-up landing. This P-38 had already suffered a landing accident in 1971. (Photo via Nicholas A. Veronico Collection)

The aftermath of the crash of c/n D.1081, N3025, #2, at Oshkosh, Wisconsin, in August 1993. (Dick Phillips)

**January 18, 1949**
C/N D.739A, NL3025 was written off in a landing accident at New Bern, North Carolina (NC). This aircraft was a G-58A civil version of the F8F-1 with all of the military hardware removed. Built for Gulf Oil, it was powered by a P&W R-2800-CA15 engine of 2,100hp; Major Al Williams (Ret.) flew it at airshows. According to a *New York Times* article dated January 19, 1949: "Al Williams' F8F crashed at the airport in New Bern, North Carolina, on January 18. Williams, unhurt, walked away from the burning wreckage. The left wheel collapsed on landing; the plane hit on its belly tank, which caught fire. The plane was a total loss."

Well-known Grumman test pilot Corwin "Corky" Meyer speculated that Williams may have failed to put the gear down.

**October 9, 1960**
C/N D.1201, N1032B was written off during a landing accident at Streator, IL, due to a loss of power while being flown by its owner, Bill Fornof. The official report reads:

> To avoid landing into the bright sun, the pilot diverted the flight to land at the alternate airport. En route to the alternate, the engine of the aircraft failed necessitating a forced landing on a beanfield. The aircraft landed wheels up, and fire, which was ignited when the external fuel tank separated, consumed the aircraft. The cause of the power failure was not determined.

April 1960 insurance records listed N1032B as having 531.6 airframe hours and 143.3 engine hours.

Fornof had only owned c/n D.1201 a short time and it is reported, at the time of the accident, he was 35 years old and had 3,500 flight hours. It is unknown how many times he had flown c/n D.1201; at the time it was struck off by the Navy it had 526 hours TT.

**August 21, 1962**
C/n D.1171, N1031B was substantially damaged during a landing at Valparaiso, IN, while on its delivery flight to its new owner. The Bearcat was flown by Richard Fennell, who had an unknown amount of fighter time but did possess a commercial pilot's

license. The ferry flight to the new owner had a scheduled fuel stop at Valparaiso and according to a local newspaper, "on an approach to the west end of the runway a witness reported the aircraft appeared to stall just above the ground where it then dropped to the ground."

Fennell reported a hydraulic failure, while others say he did not lock the tailwheel. Either way, he lost control after rolling approximately 300ft, then wobbled another 1,500ft when the Bearcat then appeared to ground-loop and began cartwheeling wing over wing until finally coming to rest inverted off the runway. Fennell was dug out from under the inverted Bearcat with only minor injuries. Later, the Bearcat was righted on its gear and towed back to a lot near the airport.

It is believed owner Tim O'Neill never flew his new Bearcat, c/n D.1171. O'Neill wrote to the FAA on February 4, 1963, requesting the civil registration be cancelled as the aircraft was being salvaged[17].

Bearcat c/n D.1171 was involved in another landing accident in June 1976. Now registered as N777L, Race #77 suffered an engine failure while attempting to qualify at the 1976 California National Air Races at Mojave, CA. An oil line separated during the qualifying run causing the engine to seize at about 500ft in altitude. After lining up to land, the gear only partly extended and N777L slid down the runway on its prop and tailwheel in a shower of sparks[18]. The damage was sufficient to keep Race #77 out of racing until 1980.

**August 13, 1966**
C/n D.1073, N7826C was written off at Amarillo Air Force Base, Amarillo, TX, while performing an aerobatic routine during the Aviation Days airshow. According to the local newspaper:

> Mr. Shelby M. Kritser, a well-known veteran Amarillo flier, crashed and died before a crowd of about 2,000 persons. His World War Two Grumman F8F Bearcat knifed into the edge of a runway and exploded in an orange-red ball of roaring flame. The tragedy occurred at 2:52pm about 200 yards from two grandstands crowded with persons on hand for the aerial demonstrations. Kritser, 52, who was president of Tradewind Aviation and chairman of the

---

17  Thankfully it wasn't

18  The author witnessed this accident while standing next to the runway. I think that if it had not been for Lyle Shelton's skill as a pilot, it could have been more serious

Texas Aeronautics Commission, completed a series of intricate and difficult maneuvers with the plane before attempting the one which cost him his life–a hammerhead stall. Krister[19] brought the Navy fighter low over the field and went into a vertical climb, executing a 360-degree roll as he approached stalling speed. At the top of the stall, he slid off into a fluttering spin with his power off. He was able to recover from the spin, but his 2,350hp [actually 2,000hp] Pratt & Whitney engine apparently failed him and he could not recover from the dive.

The NTSB report (FTW67A0024) states Shelby Kritser had 7,657 total hours and 46 hours in type. The report reads: "Pilot in command–misjudged altitude–failed to obtain/maintain flying speed–improperly executed low-altitude aerobatic maneuver, insufficient altitude–for proper spin recovery, as probable cause. Fire after impact."

In June 1970 the FAA notified William Fuller, the co-owner of c/n D.1073, of its intention to revoke the registration of N7825C for failure to submit an Aircraft Registration Eligibility, Identification, Activity Report for several years and sent Fuller a registration cancellation form. Fuller completed and returned the form. The FAA wrote back and stated that both Fuller and Kritser must sign the cancellation form as both were the registered owners. Fuller sent a letter to the FAA explaining that Kritser was unable to sign the form as he had died in the crash of N7826C in August of 1966. The FAA cancelled the registration number July 14, 1970.

## April 18,1967

C/n D.963, N5555H was destroyed while flown by Norwood R. Hanson near South Spafford, NY. Hanson was 42 years old with 5,284 total hours, 407 hours in type and not instrument rated.

Hanson was billed as "The Flying Professor and His Magnificent Flying Machine" and was a renowned author and professor with degrees from Columbia, Oxford, and Cambridge; he taught at Yale. He had flown F4U Corsairs with Marine Corps squadron VMF-452 during World War Two and regularly flew a T-6 trainer.

Hanson made the airshow circuit doing an aerobatic routine in his Bearcat, sometimes with fellow Bearcat pilot Chester Christopher. It is reported that Hanson was preparing for a world speed record attempt.

Bearcat c/n D.963 was written off on its way to Ithaca, NY, when it flew into a mountainside trying to fly visual flight rules (VFR) in instrument flight rules (IFR)

conditions. The NTSB Rreport (NYC67A0144) states probable cause as: "Pilot in Command–inadequate preflight preparation and/or planning–continued VFR flight into adverse weather conditions–low ceiling and fog. Fire after impact. Remarks–Altimeter set on 29.74in, actual value was 29.64in, pilot not instrument rated." The Bearcat was deregistered by the FAA on October 18, 1973.

## August 23, 1968

C/n D.988, N7957C was substantially damaged during a gear-up landing after an engine failure at Rebel Field, Mercedes, TX, while flown by Lloyd Nolen. The pilot was not seriously injured. This was the first F8F associated with the Confederate Air Force (now the Commemorative Air Force).

Nolen was listed as a Commercial Flight Instructor. He was 45 years old with 8,600 hours TT and 155 hours in type. According to the NTSB report (FTW69D0268): "Type of Accident–engine failure or malfunction–wheels up. PIC did not have time to fully extend gear. Probable cause: Powerplant failure for undetermined reasons–complete power loss." The remains were stored at Mercedes, TX.

In May 1970 a letter was sent to the FAA requesting the registration be cancelled at the owners' request due to the aircraft being destroyed. In a letter to the FAA on August 21, 1968, two days before the accident, the owners stated c/n D.988 had 870 hours TT for the airframe but listed nothing for the engine. Again, it is fortunate that the Bearcat was not destroyed or scrapped.

## April 26, 1969

C/n D.628, N7247C was cruising on its delivery flight to Truax Field, WI, the engine malfunctioned and pilot Ernie Savino was forced to make an emergency landing near Madison, Wisconsin (WI), short of the airport. With the gear down, he hit soft ground in a swamp and nosed over, crushing the canopy. Savino was hanging upside down, but a quick response by a passer-by saved him by cutting a hole in the fuselage. He escaped with minor injuries. Savino was an airline transport pilot, age 43, with 12,647 hours TT and ten hours in type.

The NTSB report (CHI69D0607) lists c/n D.628 as "destroyed with probable cause as: Engine failure or malfunction for undetermined reasons–forced landing off airport, on landing–landed in swamp."

---

19  Note spelling, all paperwork uses Kritser

This was the second accident for c/n D.628 as it experienced a gear-up landing in Bryan, OH, in early 1964 and was repaired.

New owner John J. Mark sent a letter to the FAA in July 1969 requesting the cancelation of the registration due to the aircraft being destroyed. What was considered "destroyed" in 1969 we now call "substantially damaged." The remains were kept and were passed around for a number of years.

**June 5, 1971**[20]

C/n D.982, N7700C suffered a wing separation during an aerobatic routine and was destroyed on impact and subsequent fire. Renowned airshow pilot William "Bill" Fornof was fatally injured. The accident happened at NAS Quonset Point, Rhode Island (RI), about ten minutes into the performance by Bill Fornof and his son Corkey, who was in another F8F. According to reports at the time, the Bearcat hit extreme wind shear that caused the wing to fail inboard of the landing gear attachment point.

An official report and the NTSB report (NYC71FNA60) stated:

At an approximate 350Kt airspeed, wingman reported heavy buffeting, negative 7.8G, positive 6.5G. Spar broke at exact CG point (middle). The Bearcat was one of two F8Fs performing a dual airshow routine. The plane was recovering from a dive at high speed when one wing failed owing to stress of 7.5G, not metal fatigue, and detached from airframe. The Bearcat crashed in a wooded area off Quonset Point NAS road, about 1.5 miles from the Naval Air Station. Probable cause: Upper cap strip fatigued–Overload failure–Separation in flight.

The aircraft's registration was cancelled by the FAA on September 1, 1971, as "aircraft totally destroyed." On May 10, 1971, c/n D.982 had 1,670.4 hours TT.

Bill Fornof flew fighters in the United States Navy during World War Two and in Korea. He had 7,700 hours TT and was 46 years old.

**April 19, 1974**

C/n D.1227, N7825C suffered substantial damage when its 50-year-old pilot with 8,000 hours TT and 386 hours in type made a forced landing "off airport" near Riviera, TX. The NTSB report (FTW74DRG78) states: "In flight normal cruise–engine failure or malfunction–

nose over on landing on rough/uneven terrain. Probable cause: PIC–inadequate preflight preparation–mismanagement of fuel–inattentive to fuel supply–fuel exhaustion. Remarks–fuel tank empty, no evidence of spillage."

Bearcat c/n D.1227 also had a minor accident on April 19, 1984, but the specifics are unknown.

**June 18, 1980**

C/n D.1125, N9885C, was destroyed near Commerce, GA, after flying into a thunderstorm and losing the left wing and breaking up. A fire occurred on impact. Owner Charles "Chub" Smith was fatally injured. Smith was 42 years old with 1,000 hours TT and a reported 400 hours in type and instrument rated.

On its last annual inspection, c/n D.1125 had 974.3 hours TT. In the post-accident NTSB report (ATL81FA055) under remarks was the following information: "Right aileron out of balance, several coats of paint–pilot aware of severe aileron flutter–hole drilled in lower wing spar." Probable cause: "PIC-continued flight into known areas of severe turbulence–exceeded designed stress limits of aircraft–attempted operation with known deficiencies in equipment."

The aircraft was deregistered October 15, 1981, by the FAA, as it was totally destroyed.

**August 1, 1993**

C/n D.1081[21] (as c/n D.739A) NL3025 had an engine malfunction on take-off from Oshkosh, WI, and made a gear-down landing in a field and then cartwheeled on impact. The Bearcat broke in half behind the canopy. Owner Elmer Ward was only slightly injured. He reported 2,256 hours TT with 56 hours in type.

The NTSB report (CHI93FA296) stated:

The Bearcat impacted approximately one-half mile off the departure end of runway 18 in an open field. During impact, the landing gear collapsed and was torn from the airframe. The pilot stated that the airplane cartwheeled clockwise on the main landing gear and right wing, followed by the engine and left wing. Ward was trapped inside until freed by rescuers. Examination of the cockpit controls… showed the throttle was full forward, the mixture and propeller controls were approximately mid-range, the mixture control was near the idle cut-off position. Further examination failed to reveal any anomalies. Probable cause: PIC inadvertent use of the mixture resulting in a lean mixture.

---

20  The reporting of this accident was overshadowed at the time as it happened the same day as the tragic Cape May, NJ fatal T-6 racing accident that killed four pilots

21  I use c/n D.1081 for this current registration as the Bearcat was restored re-using the majority of this aircraft. See photos of c/n D.1081 remains

The pilot stated that shortly after take-off (altitude of 75–100ft AGL), the engine lost power and did not respond to control inputs. He stated that he could not account for the mid-range location of the mixture control as found at the accident site. The engine had accumulated 78 hours in service since overhaul.

## May 26, 1995

C/n D.18, N9G had an emergency off-airport landing near Columbia, MO, that damaged its propeller, engine and landing gear. This necessitated it being trucked back to its home in Kalamazoo, MI. There is no NTSB report for this accident, only an FAA report, which stated "Engine malfunction/fuel malfunction–off airport landing."

## July 29, 1999

C/n D.10, N14HP was involved in an accident at Oshkosh, WI, and received substantial damage after being struck by an F4U-4 Corsair while waiting to take-off. Owner/pilot Howard Pardue was not injured.

At the time of the collision, the Bearcat was preparing to be part of an all-naval-aircraft flying display during the Experimental Aircraft Association (EAA) annual airshow/fly-in. Pardue was the flight leader aircraft in the formation, accompanied by c/n D.779, N2209, and had taxied down runway 18 approximately 1,400ft, turned toward the south-west and stopped. Approximately four seconds later, the lead aircraft of the second section, the Corsair, collided with c/n D.10, which spun around 180 degrees and off the runway into the grass. The Corsair pilot, Laird Doctor, was seriously injured and the aircraft was destroyed. Bearcat c/n D.10, which remained upright, was damaged with the right wing bent downward 40 degrees and broken aft longitudinally through the main spar, approximately 72in outboard of the wing root. The inboard wing section was also bent forward, and all four propeller blades showed heavy damage. Examination of the airplane's engine, engine controls, and other systems revealed no anomalies.

The NTSB report (CHI99FA266) listed probable cause as: "The pilot (Corsair) not following the instructions briefed by the formation leader, and pilot not maintaining clearance from the formation lead airplane."

## September 26, 1999

C/n D.1126, N800H had a minor landing accident (ground-loop) at Sacramento, CA. It was reported only as an FAA incident and the damage was "quickly and easily repaired."

## April 4, 2012

C/n D.10, N14HP collided with trees and terrain during a low-altitude aerobatic maneuver performed shortly after take-off from the Stephens County Airport, Breckenridge, TX. The commercial-rated pilot and owner was fatally injured. Thus, the life of one of the greatest Bearcat pilots came to an end. Howard Pardue and c/n D.10 had thrilled thousands of people during hundreds of airshows. Pardue was a great friend and superb pilot with more than 2,000 hours in Bearcats, who lovingly cared for c/n D.10 for more than 29 years. Bearcat c/n D.10 was substantially damaged and a post-impact fire ensued.

According to the NTSB report: (CEN12LA227):

A witness to the accident reported that he was in his airplane preparing to depart when the accident airplane was taxiing toward runway 17. The accident pilot reportedly announced over the radio that he was going to perform a Half Cuban Eight aerobatic maneuver after take-off and then overfly the runway in the opposite direction. The witness stated that after take-off the accident airplane climbed about 150ft in a shallow climb before it pitched-up into a near vertical climb. The airplane continued the climb in an outside loop before leveling out, inverted, about 500ft above the runway, heading in the opposite direction of the take-off. The witness then saw the airplane's wings roll suddenly before the airplane entered a near vertical descent. The witness described the final portion of the aerobatic maneuver as a split-S maneuver, or a descending half-loop, from which the airplane did not recover before impacting the terrain on a south-easterly heading. The witness stated that the airplane exploded on impact and a post-impact fire ensued.

Another witness reported seeing the airplane pitch-up into a steep climb shortly after take-off. The airplane continued in the steep climb to about 1,000ft above the runway where it entered a right descending roll. The witness stated that the airplane was rolling toward wings level when it descended into trees located off the south end of runway 17. The witness noted that the airplane appeared to be recovering from a dive when it impacted terrain.

The post-accident examination of the airplane revealed no evidence of mechanical malfunctions or failures that would have precluded normal operation.

The final NTSB report states: "It could not be determined if the pilot was impaired or incapacitated by an acute coronary event during the low-altitude aerobatic maneuver. Probable cause: the pilot's loss of airplane control during a low-altitude aerobatic maneuver."

Howard Pardue and c/n D.10 are greatly missed.

**August 29, 2020**
C/n D.1162, N68RW was involved in a minor taxiing incident at Wheeler Air Force Base, Hawaii (HI). While taxiing in after a flyby, the Bearcat struck a ramp portable fire extinguisher, causing the prop to throw a blade that struck a T-6G, causing damage to this aircraft's fuselage. It was repaired and is currently flyable.

As said previously, it is my belief human error was the cause of these accidents. Bearcat c/n D.963, N5555H did not fly into a mountain in bad weather, the pilot in command did. The pilot in command made the decision to fly c/n D.902, N212KA with a sick engine, or when the Bearcat was mechanically unsound, as with c/n D.988, N7957C. With the exception of c/n D.982, N7700C, the other 16 accidents can be attributed to unsound judgement by the pilot(s) in command.

I do not believe the Bearcat deserves its killer reputation any more than any other aircraft. Like any machine, boat, car, motorcycle or bicycle, failure to maintain mechanical soundness, original configuration, or control can be deadly.

C/n D.982, N7700C, taxiing out to begin a dual airshow routine with Mustang N9149R. Both were owned by Bill Fornof in April 1969. N7700C was written off in June 1971 and N9149R in December 1972 while flown by its new owner. (Robert F. Pauley)

# Flying the Bearcat

What is it like to fly Grumman's Red Hot Cat? I asked the distinguished air-race pilot Bruce Lockwood that question. Lockwood won two Championship Gold races at Reno in 1998 and 1999. He has flown for movies, for testing flights, and is a well-known warbird restorer and airshow performer. Lockwood has flown both -1 and -2 Bearcats along with Mustangs, Spitfires, Hellcat, Bf-109, Zero, P-47 and replica Yak fighters.

Pilot report by Bruce Lockwood:

### Flying

All it takes is one flight in order to be smitten by Grumman's ultimate piston-powered fighter, the legendary F8F Bearcat. An hour in the air piloting this beauty imparts the overwhelming impression that this airplane is in a league of its own. The first time you see one in person you're immediately struck by how big the propeller is and how tall, short-coupled and muscular it appears. It could be called the Mike Tyson of piston fighters. So, what's it like to fly?

Access to the cockpit is gained on the left side with steps and hand holds and, once settled in, you're quick to realize this is the best cockpit layout of any World War Two fighter. Levers, gauges and switches are well arranged and easily accessed or monitored. The seating positions set you high in the fuselage so the visibility is exceptional through the bubble canopy. You have a slight laid-back feel in the seat with ample leg clearance through all range of control stick motion.

With the pre-flight checklist complete, it's time to fire up the P&W R-2800 on F8F-1 N41089. Closing the canopy at this point will keep oil droplets and smoke from entering the cockpit during the start-up. Engaging the starter rotates the four-blade 12ft 7in diameter Aeroproducts propeller at a leisurely pace. After 12 blades pass, the Mags are switched ON and primer held ON from 4–10 seconds. As the engine begins to fire and gains rpm, the mixture lever is advanced to RICH. A little juggling is required between the mixture lever, primer button and throttle to get the big radial cleaned out and idling smoothly. The R-2800 displays a more muted exhaust note in its F8F installation as compared to the ear-shattering crescendo it produces while housed in the F4U-4 Corsair or F6F-5 Hellcat.

It takes but a slight increase in rpm to 700 or so to get the Bearcat underway. Taxiing for take-off, you appreciate the forward visibility in comparison to its naval contemporaries.

Though you still need slight S turns as you taxi to restrain from shredding a shiny Cessna, it's not the compulsory snake-dance performance required to safely taxi a Corsair.

After my safety checks, I get cleared for take-off, taxi into position and hold. With the brakes held hard and the stick in my lap, I advance the throttle to 30in of manifold pressure (MP) then lean back in the seat to get a clear view down each side of the fuselage. Peering through the shimmering heat waves generated by the exhaust being pumped by the R-2800 through 2½in dia. exhaust stacks exiting five to a side, I locate both edges of the runway for visual reference. They will be my guide to keep the F8F straight until the tail comes up.

Upon releasing the brakes and advancing the throttle, you are surprised at the lack of torque. The Bearcat starts to head slightly right initially instead of the usual left that most fighters exhibit. This is easily corrected with slight left rudder. From that point on, the Bearcat runs true down the runway with but a slight correction needed. With the throttle at 51in (Manifold Pressure (MP) @ 2,800rpm, the big Pratt is making close to 2,000hp. With an estimate take-off weight of 7,800lb that equates to 3.9lb per hp, the sheer feel of acceleration is still embedded in my mind. The Bearcat literally catapults itself off the runway before you can even raise the tail. With the nose now pointed at the sky, the Bearcat continues to accelerate as you select gear-up just prior to exceeding its 140Kt gear speed.

Continuing a climb with the VSI pegged at 6,000ft per minute takes me clear of the airspace and confines of the airport. Leveling off at 5,000ft, I let the F8F accelerate then bring the power back to cruise setting of 30" MP @ 2,000rpm with an indicated speed of 245Kt. Spending time flying a Bearcat is probably the most fun and exciting flying you could ever do in a piston-powered airplane. From stalls to loops, Cuban Eights, rolls and Immelmann, the potent Bearcat dances to the very edges of the flight envelope.

Pointing the nose back towards the airport, my flight suit now soaked from the strain of pulling Gs, it is time to bring her in for landing. Leveling out and reducing power to 30in MP @ 1,400rpm, it becomes abundantly clear what a unique experience it is to thoroughly wring out one of the finest and rarest piston airplanes in the world.

Entering the perimeter of the airport, I set up for a landing; with Tower approval I enter at 1,000ft above ground level (AGL) for the overhead approach with mid-field break. With 250Kt indicated, I reduce power while pulling tight into a 3G left break and roll-out on the downwind. As speed slows to 220Kt, I select flaps down and then the gear at 140Kt and let the speed slow to 125Kt on the base leg. With the prop set at 2,400rpm, I joggle throttle from 18–25" of MP as I roll on to final with target speed of 95Kt then reduce to 85Kt on short final. As the numbers flash under the wings, I squeeze the throttle off and flare at the same time. You notice the elevators are very sensitive at this juncture and the landing gear feels stiff as you touch down in the three-point position. The Bearcat has a familiar Mustang feel to it and rolls straight ahead with little fanfare, though it lacks the "landing in a pile of pillows" feel the Corsair, Hellcat and Skyraider poses. The taxi back to the hangar is equally easy. Rolling to a stop and running up the R-2800 then bringing the throttle back to idle you let it stabilize at 600rpm before pulling the mixture to cut-off. As the engine slows, its roaring exhaust allows you to hear the distinct clatter of the valves and the wheezing of exhaust pipes. Taking a breath, I bask in the pungent smell of hot unburnt oil and gaze through the oil droplets and bugs splattered on the wind screen. I gather my thoughts; the Bearcat has unprecedented maneuverability, buttery smooth flight controls, outstanding climb and acceleration. It is, for sure, the most balanced fighter I've ever flown. It has to be the ultimate dog fighter or airshow performer. It's over-powered, light on the controls and extremely maneuverable.

But, is it better than the P-51D Mustang?

Aesthetically, both are beautiful, but in different ways. The award goes to the P-51. When you look at one flying formation on your wing, no matter the angle, it exudes the beauty of an exotic Italian car. If the Bearcat was the Mike Tyson of fighter planes, thick-necked, rippling muscle, ready to take on anyone, then the Mustang had to be the Muhammad Ali, cunning, fast as lightning with great endurance.

### Environmentally
The Rolls Royce Merlin is a friendlier engine to sit behind, not much in the way of exhaust or engine heat. The R-2800, on the other hand, feels like sitting in a blast furnace sucking on the exhaust pipe of a 1952 Studebaker, though the F8F is better in this aspect than its colleagues, the Hellcat and Corsair.

### Cockpit Layout
The F8F is a generation beyond the P-51. It has a great cockpit feel almost akin to wearing a fine custom-made suit. You virtually wear the airplane as it fits like a glove.

### Flight Controls
An interesting contrast between them. Both have good control harmony and balance. In pitch, the Mustang requires 7lb of stick pull per G and tapers off at 5Gs at which point it starts to reverse, taking less and less pull to add Gs. The Bearcat requires the same initial stick pull at 7lb/G then reduces radically to 0lb at 4Gs; release the stick and it stays at 4Gs or starts to increase. The Mustang's roll rate is from 5–10 degrees per second slower than the Bearcat, below 250Kt, a speed of which the Mustang rolls at 95 degrees per second, but I've found the controls stiffen substantially approaching 400Kt. NACA test reports on the Bearcat quantified a roll rate of 60 degrees per second at 120Kt, but increases to 115 degrees per second at 310Kt. In summary, at over 250Kt the Bearcat has lighter controls than the Mustang and starts to exhibit neutral to negative stability in pitch. Both employ very effective rudders.

Having flown both the F8F-1 and F8F-2 Bearcats,[22] I could not tell the difference between the standard -1 tail and the higher -2 tail. If attempting a wave-off from an aircraft carrier with the short tail, NACA testing indicated that the pilot was employing 90 per cent of total right rudder travel to keep the nose straight. This was the reason behind the installation of the tall tail[23].

### Speeds
The Bearcat is the only fighter that can cruise effortlessly with the Mustang, but unfortunately has only half the P-51's range. The Bearcat generally has a 15Kt top speed advantage over the Mustang when below 15,000ft. At 20,000ft and above, the Mustang is in its element due to the Merlin's two-stage two-speed supercharger.

### Acceleration
No comparison, Bearcat wins this one. Note: Take-off and climb in a Bearcat feels much like the acceleration and climb angle of a lightly loaded Boeing 737 taking off, apart from the fact the Bearcat only needs 500ft or so to do it.

### Climb
No comparison here. Most published book numbers list the P-51D climb rate 3,500ft per minute and the F8F-1 at 4,500ft. In reality, a civilian Mustang at take-off is closer to 3,900ft/min. and the Bearcat take-off is closer to 7,000ft/min.

---

22  Bruce Lockwood flew c/n D.527, N41089, and c/n D.1126, N800H

23  Norwood Hanson installed a taller tail on c/n D.963, N5555H, during his preparation for an attempt at the world speed record

**Turn Rate**

Because of its higher power to weight ratio, the Bearcat can sustain the Gs longer in tight turns. In real combat situations, the Mustang had a higher G limit so could hold its own for a good part of the turn.

**Stalls**

The Bearcat has good stall characteristics exhibiting an increase in stick-back pressure followed by airframe buffeting at 5–10Kt before the break. The big rudder is effective in keeping the wings level as the nose drops. Speeds range from 62Kt with gear/flaps out and some power to 75Kt clean and no power. The Mustang gives less warning to the pilot prior to the break. There is a slight rumble in the airframe 3Kt or so prior to the stall that increases slightly, followed by the control stick "snatching" as the nose and left wing drops off. Speeds range between 72Kt and 86Kt, depending on a clean or dirty configuration. In general, both airplanes recover quickly with opposite rudder inputs and a release of stick-back pressure. Accelerated stalls are much more violent in both airplanes and intentional spins are not recommended in either one.

**Take-Off and Landings**

The Bearcat is easier to take-off as there is little, if any, feel of torque. Plus, the instant it breaks ground you can haul back on the stick and go straight up. My good buddy and flying partner Bob Hannah, who also flew both the Bearcat and Mustang, once stated, "If a guy had 500 hours in the F8F and had never flown a P-51, he'd bust his butt on the first flight by either going off in the runway on take-off due to torque or snap rolling when hauling back on the stick as he lifted off." For landings, I give the thumbs up to the P-51; it just feels rock solid on landing and has great brakes, a steerable tailwheel and great visibility over the nose when on the mains.

For sheer sexiness there is nothing like a fully polished P-51. That distinct sound of the Rolls-Royce Merlin is music to my ears; however, I don't think two P-51s could out-dogfight a Bearcat. There will never be another like it.

Excerpts from a letter by a Bearcat owner who flew Bearcats in naval service and as a civilian.

Flying the F8F is like having a 2,400hp Pitts. Take-off run is 300–400ft at the most and as soon as you attained 200Kt, which is approximately 3,500ft down the runway, you could pull up into a half Cuban Eight. Double Immelmanns are effortless. It is pure pilots' airplane and the F-15 and F-16 are probably the first jets built that have similar flying characteristics. Just point the way and that's where it goes. It is a fantastic airplane, the ultimate propeller driven airplane.

It's sentiment felt by everyone that has ever flown "The Last of the Red Hot Cats."

C/n D.1148, N14WB; the thrill and excitement of flying a fighter pilots' aircraft. (Jay Miller)

# Chapter 5

# INDIVIDUAL CIVIL HISTORIES

The following are the individual aircraft histories of each of the F8F Bearcats that have been civil-registered. The histories were assembled from various sources that include their United States Navy record cards and FAA registration files. While this is a civil history, I have included known military histories for a complete view of each aircraft's life. Civil histories for the most part are pieced together from FAA files covering requests by owners for modification, repairs, use applications and ownership records and only show legal recorded owners.

In some cases, an aircraft may physically change ownership several times without the paperwork reflecting the changes and there being no change to the aircraft's location or flight status. Bearcats were usually issued a Ferry Permit to allow the new owner to remove them from United States government property, or from a previous owner's location, for short flights to their eventual home airports. A General Ferry Permit would allow the following as shown by the one issued to c/n D.1105 allowing ten days to move the Bearcat:

1. This flight shall be made in accordance with visual flight rules (VFR) (Day) only, and shall be limited to personnel essential to the flight and their baggage.
2. This authorization is valid upon certification in the aircraft log book by an A&P mechanic, after inspection, that the aircraft is airworthy for this flight.
3. This permit valid for one (1) flight only and shall expire upon arrival at destination, but not later than sunset on: January 12, 1965.
4. The pilot must be properly rated and qualified.
5. This ferry authorization shall be carried in the aircraft, at all times, during flight.

Like anything written down, these record cards contain errors and omissions. I made every effort to verify accuracy. In numerous cases, Bearcats were registered under a company or corporate name or through a partnership. I included owners or the names of the known partners. Histories are current at the time of publication.

# C/N D.10

BuNo 90446, XF8F-1
Acceptance date: April 30, 1945
Delivery date: May 19, 1945

Assigned: May 1945 to Naval Air Test Center, Patuxent River, MD. August 1945 to Electrical Test at NATC. September 1945 to Tactical Test at NATC until November 1947. December 1947 to Aircraft Pool Naval Air Station Norfolk, VA. until June 1948. To Naval Air Reserve Training Unit (NART) at NAS Jacksonville, Florida (FL). To Naval Air Development Center (NADC) Johnsville, Pennsylvania (PA) in 1949. Sometime between its assignment at Jacksonville and Johnsville, it was converted to an F8F-1D drone control aircraft. (Note: BuAer record does not reflect this conversion, however, there is photographic evidence.) Stricken 1954. To Smithsonian Institution's National Air and Space Museum with date unknown. In storage disassembled at NASM until 1976 when traded to Darryl Greenamyer. Sold to Wolcott Air Service Inc, Wolcott, CT, March 1977, and registered as N99279. Restored to flying by George Enhorning/Wolcott Air Service with first flight in 1982. Sold to Howard Pardue, Breckenridge, TX, in 1983 and registration number changed to NL14HP. Registered owner changed to Breckenridge Aviation Museum in 1984. Competed as Race #14. On August 20, 1998, reported to have 2,200 hours TT on the airframe. Damaged in ground collision at Oshkosh, WI, on August 29, 1999, and subsequently rebuilt. Minor landing accident June 25, 2002. Substantially damaged in fatal crash at Breckenridge, TX, on April 4, 2012. Parts salvaged and registration canceled December 8, 2020. Last registered to Texas Bearcats LLC of Dover, Delaware (DE).

C/n D.10, BuNo 90446, the 12th XF8F-1 built and the tenth developmental aircraft at Atlantic City, New Jersey, circa 1945. Bearcat 90446 was used at the time for electrical and tactical testing at Naval Air Training Center Patuxent River, Maryland, and would survive to become a civil Cat, N99279, N14HP. (Roger Besecker)

C/n D.10 as N99279 after restoration to flying status by George Enhorning of Wolcott Air Service in 1982. Bearcat N99279 is shown wearing the markings of the commanding officer of Air Group 19 from the USS *Boxer*. (Dick Phillips)

C/n D.10 as NL14HP, owned by Howard Pardue, in August 1983. Pardue changed the markings of 90446 after purchasing the aircraft from George Enhorning. The markings shown remained unchanged throughout its flying time. (Bob Kennedy)

C/n D.10 as Race #14 at Reno in 1988 sporting a prop-spinner. Number 14 NL14HP raced at Reno and other events from 1984–2009. (Russ Hiatt)

C/n D.10 taxiing out at the Reno Air Races in September 2005. Howard Pardue and NL14HP were tragically lost at their home airport in Breckenridge, Texas, in April 2012. (Jerry Liang)

# C/N D.18

BuNo 90454, XF8F-1
Acceptance date: May 7, 1945
Delivery date: May 11, 1945

Assigned: May 1945 to Fighting Squadron Nineteen, VF-19, at Naval Air Facility Santa Rosa, CA, until July 30, 1945. In August 1945 to Fighter Bomber Squadron Eighteen, VFB-18, at NAS Alameda, CA. To Combat Aircraft Service Unit Five, CASU-5, Pool, September 1945 to September 1946. To Fleet Aircraft Service Squadron Eight, FASRON-8, Pool October 1946 until recondition at NAS Alameda November 1946 through December 1946. To NAS Alameda Pool January 1947 to December 1947 then to NAS Norfolk Pool December 1947 until June 1948. Stricken 02/04/1949. To storage NAF Litchfield Park, AZ. Sold surplus 1958 and registered N6624C. Sold to E. D. Weiner of Los Angeles, CA, on March 24, 1959, and registered as N3351. Sold in 1963 to Vernon D. Jarvis of Decatur, IL, who modified it for aerial survey work with the installation of a photo panel and a door in the right side for access of the photographer into the rear fuselage. Sold in 1964 to R.E. Schreder of Bryan, OH. Sold in 1968 to Gunther W. Balz of Kalamazoo, MI. The registration was changed to N9G in 1969 by Balz. He used it for both airshows and air racing as Race #7, for which the Bearcat was modified with the installation of a spinner and fuel cells in the outer wing panels. Sold in 1978 to Kalamazoo Aviation History Museum (Preston Parish).

This Bearcat has flown in three distinctive paint schemes: 1. red, white and gold, 2. Royal Thai Air Force and 3. standard United States navy blue. The aircraft was damaged during a forced landing in Missouri due to engine stoppage in May 1995. Repairs completed in 2001. Sold to Jens Meyerhoff of Arizona in April 2009 and currently flies almost weekly.

C/n D.18, BuNo 90454, the 18th XF8F-1 developmental aircraft registered as N3351 shown in Santa Monica, California. While owned by E. D. Wiener, the aircraft sported a two-tone red with gold stripe. (John Dzurica Sr.)

C/n D.18, N3351, at Oakland, California, in November 1959. Number 90454 was assigned to the first operational Bearcat squadron, VF-19, at Naval Auxiliary Air Station (NAAS) Santa Rosa, California, before the end of World War Two. NAAS Santa Rosa is about 60 miles north of Oakland. (Larry S. Smalley)

C/n D.18, 90454, now N9G at DuPage, Illinois, having passed through several owners. One former owner modified it for aerial survey work by adding a door on the right side in 1963. When Gunther Balz bought N9G in 1968, he removed the door and cleaned up the airframe for airshow demonstrations and air racing. (Dick Phillips Collection)

C/n D.18 at Reno, Nevada, in September 1970 as Race #7 flown by Gunther Balz. Notice the repaired area where the access door had been removed. By this time, Balz had added a prop spinner and fuel tanks in the outer wing panels for both transcontinental and pylon racing. (Emil Strasser)

C/n D.18, N9G, in Royal Thai Air Force markings while owned by the Kalamazoo Aviation History Museum at London, Ontario, Canada, in June 1984. The museum obtained N9G in 1978 from Gunther Balz. (William "Bill" Jesse)

C/n D.18, N9G, sporting the markings of VF-3A at Kalamazoo, Michigan, in 1986. It suffered a landing accident in May 1995 and made its first flight after repairs in 2001. It was sold to its current owner Jens Meyerhoff in April 2009 and is flown regularly. (Bill Painter)

C/n D.18, N9G, being tugged back to its hangar in California after a flight. Owner Jens Meyerhoff flies it almost weekly. (Jens Meyerhoff)

# C/N D.527

BuNo 95255, F8F-1
NAVAER Aircraft History Card not available.

To Mutual Defense Assistance Program, MDAP, sold to France in May 1952 and assignment to Armee de l'Air French Indochina. To Republic of South Vietnam in 1956. Noted on display at Tan Son Nhut Air Base, South Vietnam, 1966 through the 1980s. To J. Salis Aviation, La Ferte-Alais, France, c.1987, and disassembled. Sold c.1990 to Liberty Aero Corporation (David Price) of Santa Monica, CA, for rebuilding to flying and registered N65135 on September 17, 1990. Registered as N41089 in September 1994, still with Liberty Aero. First flight in 33 years at Mojave, CA, on May, 19, 1995. Change in registered owner in 1996 to Museum of Flying Support Fund of Santa Monica, CA, with David Price as Director. Competed as Race #204 from 1996–99 by Price, Alan Preston and Skip Holm. Sold in September 2000 to Tony Banta of Livermore, CA. Registration changed to N58204 in 2002. Sold to Rod Lewis of San Antonio, TX, on October 2, 2006. Currently registered to Lewis Fighter Fleet/Spitfire Ventures LLC, San Antonio, TX. Sometime between 2016 and 2022 the aircraft had a minor nose-over accident on landing. Currently flying.

C/n D.527, BuNo 95255, F8F-1, N41089, in April 1996, about one year after its first flight in approximately 33 years. The aircraft is a veteran of Indochina and was restored and flown by the Museum of Flying in Santa Monica, California. (Bob Kennedy)

C/n D.527, N41089, taxiing out in Mojave, California, in October 2000, on its delivery flight to new owner Tony Banta. Banta would change the registration to N58204 in 2002. (Bob Kennedy)

C/N. D.527 N58204 recently at San Antonio, Texas, taking off for a flight. This is one of four Bearcats owned by Warbird collector Rod Lewis of San Antonio, where it is currently based and is flyable. (Jay Miller)

# C/N D.628

BuNo 95356 F8F-1
Acceptance date: March 18, 1947
Delivery date: In delivery March 1947

To NAS Norfolk, VA, in April 1947. To VF-20A May 1947 through February 1948. To VF-152 in March 1948. Aboard the USS *Valley Forge* CV-45 with VF-152 in October 1948. To NAS Alameda, CA, with VF-152 in November 1948. To the overhaul and repair department (O&R) NAS Alameda September 9, 1949. There is no stricken date listed. Sold in November 1957 from NAS North Island, CA, for $2,029.59 to Fred A. Kessler of Hollywood, CA, and registered as N7247C. Sold to E. D. Weiner of Los Angeles, CA, in November 1957. Sold to W. F. Patterson Jr. of Roselle, IL, on the same date. Sold in March 1958 to Perry Boswell of Delray Beach, FL. Sold in November 1959 to William Eckhart of Fort Lauderdale, FL[24]. Sold in May 1960 to Vernon Jarvis of Decatur, IL. Sold in November 1962 to R. E. Schreder[25] of Bryan, OH. Minor accident on landing at Bryan, OH, repaired. Sold in October 1964 to E. J. Saviano of La Grange, IL. Sold in March 1969 for $3,595.00 to John J. Mark of Hales Corner, WI. Crashed on delivery flight while flown by Saviano on April 26, 1969, at Madison, WI, and the remains were stored there. Remains sold in April 1971 to Gunther Balz of Kalamazoo, MI, but not registered. Remains donated September 1977 to Kalamazoo Aviation History Museum. Remains sold in December 1980 to Joseph Tobul of Wexford, PA. Sold in April 1983 to Gerald Beck of Wahpeton, North Dakota (ND). Little restoration work had been done as the airframe was mostly likely used for parts. Sold in May 1983 to John Dowd Jr. of Syracuse, Kansas (KS). In December 1983, Dowd requested the FAA reinstate its registration and change the registration number to N4752Y. Dowd began slow restoration using this airframe and parts from several non-civil airframes he had recovered. He also used parts from several wrecked Bearcats as well as manufacturing

C/n D.628, BuNo 95356, F8F-1, N7247C, on the ramp at Long Beach, California, in early 1958, shortly after being removed from surplus storage at NAS North Island. Note that the aircraft's blue paint was stripped and gun ports covered, but it otherwise appears to be untouched. (John Dzurica Sr.)

some new parts and a new spar. Project sold to Texas Flying Legends Museum of Houston, TX. Shipped in 2012 to Ezell Aviation Breckenridge, TX, for work to make it flyable. Made its first flight in 50 years in 2019, but had engine trouble. It was not flown again until March 2021 and sold to Steuart Walton of Bentonville, Arkansas (AR). Currently registered to Echo Matrix LLC, Bentonville, and flyable. Reported left gear collapsed on take-off incurring a prop strike at Bentonville, AR, on October 11, 2024. Repairable.

---

24  It is very possible that during this time the Bearcat was not flown and remained parked at Long Beach, CA, awaiting a type certificate/airworthy permit

25  E. D. Weiner, Vernon Jarvis and R. E. Schreder (review of FAA record cards) had multiple connections in early Bearcat transactions

C/n D.628, N7247C, flown by Pete Finley over Fort Lauderdale, Florida, in 1960. Finley was with VF-61 aboard the USS *Coral Sea* in 1948 when VF-61 operated F8Fs. (Pete Finley)

C/n D.628, N7247C, at Bryan, Ohio, in June 1964, undergoing repairs following a gear-up landing while owned by R.E. Schreder. Note repairs to cowling and the gear doors are still bent and scrapped. The aircraft had its outer wing panels replaced by yellow ones with stars and bars from a drone-control Bearcat. (Robert F. Pauley via Bill Slate)

C/n D.628, N7247C, at Truax Field in Madison, Wisconsin, in April 1969, where it crashed on its delivery flight to a new owner. Part of the left wing is in the foreground. (Steve Stuczynski)

C/n D.628 showing the opposite side view at Madison, Wisconsin. There was extensive damage to the left side. In 1969, N7247C was not considered worth rebuilding, but fortunately its remains were stored. (Steve Stuczynski)

C/n D.628; this is what remained when Joe Tobul bought N7247C in 1980. It appears to have served as a parts airframe for other Bearcat projects. The photo was taken in July 1982 at Wexford, Pennsylvania. (Dennis Childers via Lorenz Rasse)

C/n D.628, now registered as N4752Y, changed hands a few more times before being acquired by Texas Flying Legends of Houston, Texas. Restoration work started in 2012, using a collection of parts from numerous Bearcats. (Jay Miller)

C/n D.628, N4752Y, standing on its gear and almost complete. In 2017, this Dash-1 took flight for the first since 1969. It is currently flyable with Steuart Walton's museum collection. (Jay Miller)

# C/N D.739A

BuNo None, G-58A

The first of two civil Bearcats built by Grumman as company demonstrators. The G-58A was basically an F8F-1 without military hardware. First flown by Grumman as NC1201V in April 1947. Sold in July 1947 to Gulf Oil Co, named *Gulfhawk 4th* and registration changed to NL3025. Flown by famed test pilot and airshow performer Major Alford "Al" Williams (Ret) at airshows doing aerobatics and promoting Gulf Oil products. *Gulfhawk* was destroyed in 1949. A short paragraph in the *New York Times* on January 19, 1949, read: "Al Williams' F8F crashed at the airport in New Bern, North Carolina, on January 18. Williams unhurt, walked away from the burning wreckage. The left wheel collapsed on landing; the plane hit on its belly tank, which caught fire. The plane was a total loss[26]."

C/n D.739A, no BuNo, G-58A, NL3025, the first of two civil Bearcats that were not militarized. Bearcat NL3025 was built by Grumman as a company demonstration aircraft for Gulf Oil Co and flown by airshow pilot Major Al Williams (Ret.) as *Gulfhawk 4th*. Photographed in New York in 1948. (Howard Levy via William T. Larkins)

---

26  The Bearcat currently flying with this c/n is not the same aircraft. It is only using this c/n after a change approved by the FAA. See c/n 1081 for history of the Bearcat currently using c/n 739A

C/n D.739A shown in a promotional photo given out by Gulf Oil Co. (Grumman Corp)

# C/N D.779

BuNo 122095, F8F-1B
NAVAER Aircraft History Card not available

To Mutual Defense Assistance Program, MDAP, sold to Thailand in 1952 or 1953 for use by Royal Thai Air Force. Noted on display in Bangkok, Thailand 1965–80s. Sold in 1987 to J. Salis Collection, La Ferte-Alais, France *c.*1987 and disassembled. Sold disassembled in 1988 to Stephen Gray of Duxford, England. Registered G-BUCF to the Fighter Collection Duxford at the same time. Stored from 1988–92. Sold in 1992 to Charles F. Nichols/Yanks Air Museum in Chino, CA. Arrived in Chino disassembled in April 1992 for restoration to flying and registered as N2209. First flight at Chino was in February 1999. Sold on April 1, 1999, to Quality Leasing Co of Indianapolis, IN. Tom Wood was listed as principal partner. Wood passed away in 2010 and his sons continue with his aviation foundation. Currently a regular flyer.

C/n D.779, BuNo 122095, F8F-1B, registered as N2209 at Chino, California, in May 1999 shortly after its first flight. Bearcat N2209 is another former Indochina aircraft that was returned to the United States and restored to flying. (Jerry Liang)

C/n D.779 recently at Oshkosh, Wisconsin, for the annual airshow. Bearcat N2209 has been owned by the late Tom Wood and his aviation foundation since 1999 and flies regularly. (John Steele)

# C/N D.902

BuNo 121528, F8F-2
Acceptance date: March 5, 1948
Delivery date: March 1948

To NAS Quonset Point, RI, In March 1948 with VF-8A. To VF-72 of Carrier Air Group Seven, CVG-7, in July 1948. To NAS Quonset Point with VF-72 in November 1948. To NAS Norfolk, VA, and O&R on July 8, 1949. There is no recorded stricken date.

Sold surplus July 31, 1958, for $449.64 to Texas Aviation Material Inc[27], of Dallas, TX, and registered as N9886C. In a "Bill of Sale" dated July 3, 1959, N9886C was "Mutual Traded" to John F. Carr. He sold it on December 19, 1960, to Northwest Aerial Survey Inc of Rosemount, MN. Carr was a vice president of this company. Northwest installed a camera and had the Bearcat overhauled and certified for "Aerial Photography." By June 1961, N9886C had 768 hours TT. Sold on September 7, 1962, to Kucera and Associates (Robert Kucera was principal owner) of Cleveland, OH. Aircraft modified in March 1963 for aerial survey work with "Aft facing two passenger seat installed between fuselage stations 146 and 181.5 and passenger entry door installed between stations 196.5 and 229.5. Camera installed between stations 181.5 and 213 with passenger windows installed in each side between stations 158 and 181.5. Note: passenger is defined as necessary crew to operate photographic mission." In May 1963 Kucera changed the registration to N212KA. By June 1967, N212KA had 1,230 hours TT at which time Kucera sealed the outer wing panels to carry fuel, increasing his flying time from two to four hours. Kucera raced N212KA twice during 1968 as Race #99. The first race was the Harold's Club Transcontinental Trophy Race Dash from Milwaukee to Reno, placing fourth. Then he raced it at Reno during the National Championship pylon races placing first in the Consolation Race. N212KA was written off in a double fatal accident, Bob Kucera and a passenger being killed, on December 12, 1968, at Willoughby, OH, due to engine failure. In 1969, the outer wing panels were sold to Lyle Shelton of Los Alamitos, CA, along with other parts. Registration was cancelled on June 25, 1973. By the 1980s, the remains had been sold to Joseph Tobul of Wexford, PA. In 1983, the remains went to John Dowd of Syracuse, KS, with intent to rebuild it to flying condition using various wrecks and new manufactured parts. About 2012, Texas Flying Legends acquired the remaining parts for possible use in a project. The remains have been used in several restoration projects over the years.

C/n D.902, BuNo 121528, F8F-2 as N9886C, possibly photographed during its civil conversion in October 1960 at Minneapolis, Minnesota, before modification for aerial survey work. (Dick Phillips Collection.)

---

27 One of two that Texas Aviation Material Inc bought that day, both for the same price. The other was c/n D.1125

*Above*: C/n D.902, N212KA, left side showing the window for the camera operator, a modification completed in 1963 by Kucera; its airworthiness certificate stated, "Passenger is defined as necessary crew to operate photographic mission." (Dick Phillips Collection)

*Opposite*: C/n D.902 now registered as N212KA of Kucera & Associates, Cleveland, Ohio, in about 1966. Seen in this photo are the fuselage window and door added for a camera operator who sat in the aft fuselage area. The door was on the right side. (Dick Phillips Collection)

C/n D.902 was modified again in 1967 by Kucera, who sealed the outer wing panels for fuel storage to extend the flight range from two hours to four. Photo shows N212KA at the Reno Air Races in 1968 where it had raced in the transcontinental and pylon races as Race #99. (William T. Larkins)

C/n D.902, N212KA, upon return to Ohio in September 1968, still wearing its race number. It would fatally crash in December 1968. Parts of this Bearcat have been used over the years to help restore other Bearcats. (Dick Phillips Collection)

# C/N D.963

BuNo 121589 F8F-2
Acceptance date: April 22, 1948
Delivery date: April 1948

To NAS Quonset Point, RI, in April 1948 to VF-72 (VF-8A was originally written but was crossed out). Aboard the USS *Leyte*, CV-32, with VF-72 September–October 1948. Returned to NAS Quonset Point with VF-72 in November 1948. With Marine Aircraft Engineering Squadron Twelve, AES-12, MCAS Quantico, VA, in October 1951. There is no Stricken date. Sold as surplus on December 29, 1958, to Hemet Valley Flying Service of Hemet, CA, for $640.00 and registered N5171V. Sold on February 17, 1959, to Clifford S. Hatfield of Imperial, CA, for "aerial survey work with the civil conversion work being done by Acme Aircraft." Hatfield repaired

N5171V including "Belly of fuselage repaired from Sta.229.1/2 aft to Sta. 262.1/2 and between Stringers #10R and #10L by repairing damaged bulkheads and skin. Access door repaired. Landing gear retraction checked." The final date of these repairs was April 5, 1961. Sold on October 2, 1961, to R. L. Brongersma c/o Desert Aviation Inc of Phoenix, AZ, with 610 hours TT for $10.00 and other valuable consideration (OVC). Sold on April 2, 1962, to Norwood R. Hanson of Bloomington, IN, again for $10.00 and OVC. Re-registered in 1964 as N5555H by Hanson with 710 hours TT. Hanson flew the Bearcat for an airshow aerobatic routine billed as "The Flying Professor and His Magnificent Flying Machine." For this routine, he added wing-tip end plates just outboard of the ailerons, augmented the height of the tail and rudder and squared it at the top. He and fellow Bearcat owner Chester Christopher performed a dual Bearcat aerobatic routine. Bearcat N5555H was written off on April 18, 1967, near South Spafford, NY, while flying in instrument flight rules (IFR) weather. Hanson was fatally injured. The Bearcat was de-registered by the FAA on October 18, 1973.

C/n D.963, BuNo 121589, F8F-2 registered as N5171V and painted a glossy red at New Haven, Connecticut, in July 1964. Owned by Norwood R. Hansen, the aircraft sports the wing end plates installed for his aerobatic routine. (Doug Slowiak)

C/n D.963, now registered N5555H, in November 1965 with a more dramatic paint scheme in the form of a hawk. Notice the talons down the landing gear; its color was reported as red and cream. (Tom Cuddy via Dusty Carter)

C/n D.963 photo shows N5555H with its taller squared-off tail and rudder. Hansen billed himself as the "Flying Professor and His Magnificent Flying Machine." The Bearcat was written off in a fatal crash on April 18, 1967. (Dick Phillips Collection)

# C/N D.982

BuNo 121608 F8F-2P
Acceptance date: May 28, 1948
Delivery date: On delivery to NAS Norfolk, VA, in May 1948

To Pool Acceptance and Test (A&T), NAS Quonset Point, RI, in July 1948. To VF-173 at NAS Quonset Point in October 1948. No further record until sold surplus on May 26, 1958, to E. D. Weiner for $1,367.01 and registered as N7700C[28]. Sold 0n July 7, 1958, to Grover Collins of Bakersfield, CA, with 691.2 hours TT. Sold on September 26, 1960, to J. W. "Bill" Fornof[29] of Houma, LA, having only flown 1.45 hours while owned by Collins. Fornof used it on the airshow circuit doing an aerobatics routine and naval-style take-offs and landings later alongside his son in G-58B. By May 10, 1971, N7700C had accumulated 1,670.4 hours TT. Bearcat N7700C was written off during an airshow at NAS Quonset Point, RI, on June 5, 1971, when, during a high-speed pull-up, the wing failed. Registration was cancelled by the FAA on September 1, 1971, as "aircraft totally destroyed." Pieces of this aircraft have been used to restore and maintain several other Bearcats.

---

28  It appears, based on original paperwork filed with the FAA, this was the first F8F-2 Bearcat licensed for civil use. See Chapter 6

29  Fornof already owned c/n D.1201

C/n 982, BuNo 121608, F8F-2P, was the first Bearcat to be licensed for the civil market. Grover Collins registered N7700C on July 7, 1958, before the aircraft was sold September 26, 1960, to world renowned aerobatic pilot J. W. "Bill" Fornof. He painted it in a Cadillac gold/bronze paint scheme. It is shown at the Lancaster, California, air races in 1965, but it did not race. (Emil Strasser)

C/n D.982, N7700C, at Milwaukee, Wisconsin, in August 1968, preparing for the start of Fornof's airshow routine. Bearcat c/n D.982 was one of three F8F-2Ps that made it on to the civil rolls. (Dick Phillips)

C/n D.982 seen at NAS Corpus Christi, Texas, in June 1970. The Bearcat would be written off in a fatal crash a year later at NAS Quonset Point, Rhode Island, on June 5, 1971. In an eerie note, c/n D.982 had been assigned to VF-173 at Naval Air Station Quonset Point during its naval service. (Pete Bulban)

# C/N D.988

BuNo 121614 F8F-2
Acceptance date: April 30, 1948
Delivery date: In delivery April 1948 to NAS Norfolk, VA

To Pool NAS Quonset Point, RI, in May 1948. To VF-62 at NAS Norfolk in August 1948. To NAS Oceana, VA, with VF-62 in September 1948. To O&R NAS Norfolk in October 1948. To NAS Norfolk with VF-62 in November 1948. Notation as stricken, but no date. Sold as surplus on August 1, 1958, at NAS North Island, CA, for $755.00 to John M. Wells[30] of Mercedes, TX, and registered as N7957C. Registered in February 1959 to Bearcat and Company of Mercedes, TX. John M. Wells and L. P. Nolen of Mercedes are listed as co-owners of Bearcat and Co in a March 1960 letter to the FAA requesting an "Experimental Classification to conduct exploratory or research flights to determine the aircraft capabilities in aerobatics." The request was granted. On March 22, 1960, Bearcat and Co reported to the FAA that there were 726.4 hours TT on the airframe and 495.0 hours TT on engine[31]. In May 1961, a letter was sent to the FAA requesting a 12-month Experimental Airworthiness Certificate for "Limited Exhibition." The request was granted. In July 1962, a request was made for change in ownership for Bearcat and Co with Marvin L. Gardner and L.P. Nolen of Mercedes as co-owners. On May 17, 1963, Bearcat and Co reported to the FAA a total of 803 hours for the airframe and 572 hours TT engine. On August 21, 1968, Bearcat and Co reported to the FAA 870 hours TT for airframe. On August 23, 1968, N7957C was heavily damaged in a take-off accident while flown by Nolen, who was not seriously injured. Remains were stored at Mercedes. In a May 1970 letter to the FAA was a request

C/n D.988, BuNo 121614, F8F-2, N7957C, in the original Confederate Air Force (CAF) color scheme in May 1963. It is one of three Bearcats associated with the CAF over the years. (Dick Phillips Collection)

to cancel the registration at owners' request due to aircraft being destroyed. From 1986 to 1992, the remains, still in the United States, were held by Stephen Grey/Fighter Collection of Duxford, England. The remains moved to Chino, CA. In 1992, Steve Hinton and company began a 14-year slow rebuild to flight status. It was sold in 2008 to Rod Lewis of San Antonio, TX, and registered in April 2009 as N747NF. First flight at Chino was May 6, 2009. Currently registered to Spitfire Ventures of San Antonio. Last known to have flown in early 2024. Flyable.

---

30  One of two John M. Wells purchased on this date. The other being c/n D.1148. Both are now with the Rod Lewis Collection

31  It would seem that the US Navy overhauled the engine on c/n D.988 sometime before it was placed into storage, which was a lucky deal for its new owners

C/n D.988 as it would have looked before being heavily damaged in a take-off accident on August 23, 1968. Fortunately, the remains of N7957C were stored. (Pete Bulban via Jay Miller)

C/n D.988 in September 2009 at Reno, Nevada, after restoration as NX747NF. The remains were passed around for years until they were hauled to Chino, California, for rebuild by Steve Hinton and company. In May 2009, c/n D.988 made its first flight after restoration. (Bob Kennedy)

It took 14 years to restore c/n D.988. Bearcat NX747NF was sold to Rod Lewis in 2008 and is currently registered to Spitfire Ventures. It is taking off from its home base at San Antonio, Texas, NX747NF, and looks fantastic. (Jay Miller)

# C/N D.1020

BuNo 121646 F8F-2
Acceptance date: June 18, 1948
Delivery date: In delivery June 1948 to NAS Norfolk, VA

To Pool A&T NAS Quonset Point, RI, in July 1948. To VF-62 at NAS Norfolk in August 1948. With VF-62 to NAS Oceana, VA, in September 1948. With VF-62 at NAS Norfolk in November 1948. Stricken date not legible. Sold as surplus by NAS North Island, CA, in 1959 to Antelope Valley Aerial Survey Co of Palmdale, CA, and registered as N7699C.

Aircraft does not show evidence of modification for survey work. In 1964, Antelope Valley Aerial Survey Co changed the registration number to N1111L. Sold in 1965 to Darryl G. Greenamyer of Monrovia, CA. Greenamyer modified the aircraft for air racing until it became one of the most highly modified racers ever built. It competed as Race #1. In 1970, the registered owner changed to Fighter Aircraft Museum Inc of Mission Hills, CA, of which Greenamyer has a close "association." On August 16, 1969, Greenamyer and N1111L set a new 3km world speed record of 482.462mph at Edwards Air Force Base, CA. *N1111L* successfully raced from 1964 to 1975[32]. In 1976, Greenamyer traded N1111L to the National Air and Space Museum for Bearcat 90446. It is currently on display with the NASM in Washington, D.C.

C/n D.1020, BuNo 121646, F8F-2, N1111L, in stock civil condition at Lancaster, California, on May 5, 1961. At that time, N1111L was registered to Antelope Valley Aerial Survey of Palmdale, California, and was bare metal overall and registered in the "Restricted" category. (Dusty Carter)

---

32  See Chapter Seven for racing details

C/n D.1020, N1111L, at Flabob Airport in Riverside County, California, in January 1964, still unmodified and for sale. Barely visible are the remains of the "Restricted" category markings below the canopy. Insignia on the cowling appears to be a stylized F-104. (Emil Strasser)

C/n D.1020, N1111L, was transformed into a dedicated racer by May 1966 at the Lancaster, California, air races. (Emil Strasser)

By September 1970, c/n D.1020 was a world-record holder and race-winning champion. Bearcat N1111L at Reno, Nevada, sports an overall gloss white paint scheme. (Jerry Liang)

C/n D.1020 at the 1972 Reno races flown by Richard Laidley, while Darryl Greenamyer sat out two suspensions for violation of a racing rule in 1971. Laidley was the fastest qualifier at 411.189mph. (William T. Larkins)

C/n D.1020 in May 1973 at Mojave, California. Bearcat N1111L did not race in 1973 due to Greenamyer's suspension. (John Stewart)

DARRYL GREENAMYER
American Jet
NIIIL
AIRCRAFT CYLINDER

*Opposite*: C/n D.1020 in one of the most remarkable paint schemes carried by a Bearcat. At the Mojave, California, races in 1975, N1111L was sponsored by American Jet Industries of Van Nuys, California. Greenamyer would finish third in the Championship race. (Bob Kennedy)

*Right*: C/n D.1020 as it was tugged out at Mojave, California, in 1975. At Reno it would qualify at 435.566mph. This was a new world record for closed-course pylon racing for piston engine aircraft. The year 1975 would be N1111L's last year to race. It had six Gold race wins at Reno, but engine problems kept it out of the Championship race. Darryl Greenamyer would trade it to the National Air and Space Museum where it is on display. (Russ Hiatt)

# C/N D.1053

BuNo 121679 F8F-2
Acceptance date: July 27, 1948
Delivery date: In delivery July 1948 to NAS Norfolk, VA

To Pool A&T NAS Quonset Point, RI, in September 1948. To VF-61 at NAS Norfolk in October 1948. To AES-12 at MCAS Quantico, VA, in October 1951. Stricken date illegible. Sold as surplus at NAS North Island, CA, on May 27, 1958, to Tucker Aircraft Sales in San Jose, CA, for $1,177.00 and registered N4992V. Sold on June 16, 1958, to Eunice C. Pierce of Saratoga, CA. Sold on November 12, 1959, to Altair Aviation Co (Eugene H. Akers) of Oxnard, CA. Sold on May 6, 1960, to Charles A. O. Hanlon of Weather Modification Co in San Jose, CA. Hanlon planned to modify it for use in "cloud-seeding" operations, although there is no evidence that it was modified. Aircraft had 854.9 hours TT at time of sale. Sold on January 27, 1962, to Bud Marquis of Marysville, CA. Sold on May 13, 1963, to Naylor Aviation of California of Oakland, CA. Sold on consignment June 4, 1963, to Larry Hamilton, dba Hamilton Aircraft Sales, of Sonoma, CA, for $6,000.00. Hamilton damaged the aircraft at Monterey, CA[33], in a minor ground-loop accident. Repossessed on March 25, 1964, by Appliance Buyers Credit Corp of St. Joseph, MI, the aircraft's registered owner after a failed deal by Hamilton to sell the Bearcat to Thomas Mathews of Monterey, CA. Sold at auction on April 6, 1964, to Michael Coutches of Hayward, CA, and reregistered as N818F on April 6, 1964. Reported as having 1,006 hours TT on October 13, 1965. It appeared at the 1967 Reno Air Races but did not compete. Stored in Hayward, CA, and owned by Coutches for 58 years. It was sold to Walter Bowe of Sonoma, CA, in June 2022 for restoration to flight. Currently under restoration. This Bearcat has spent its entire civilian life in California. Listed for sale on 16 September 2024.

---

33  Bearcats had once been stationed at the Naval Post Graduate School in Monterey, CA

C/n D.1053, BuNo 121679, F8F-2, N4992V, was surplus in 1959. It still wore its faded military Navy paint scheme and stenciling when photographed at Marysville, California, in June 1964. Notice the wing gun ports have been covered. While owned by Weather Modification Co, there was a proposal to modify the Bearcat for cloud-seeding work. (Russ Hiatt)

C/n D.1053, now registered as N818F, and painted bright yellow with black trim, at Hayward, California, in 1973. This Bearcat has not been flown in 56 years and was only seen outside on days when its hangar needed cleaning and an occasional airshow days. (John Stewart)

C/n D.1053, N818F on its way to a new life and a chance to fly again. Sold to Walt Bowe in June 2022, by July it is on its way to Sonoma, California, for restoration. Note that only the prop and outer wing panels needed to be removed to make N818F transportable. (Tony Derrer)

# C/N D.1073

BuNo 121699 F8F-2
Acceptance date: August 20, 1948
Delivery date: In delivery August 1948
to NAS San Diego, CA

To Pool NAS San Diego in September 1948. To Pool NAS Alameda, CA, in October 1948. To NAS Jacksonville, FL, Reserve Squadron with date unknown. Stricken. Sold as surplus August 15, 1958, to Acme Aircraft Parts Inc[34], of Compton, CA, for $611.99 with 490.5 hours TT. Sold August 20, 1958, to John W. and Mary W. Dorr of Orinda, CA, for $1,100.00 for the purpose of "aerial photography." Photographed at Concord, CA, in October 1958 with registration number N7826C, painted over Navy markings. According to FAA records, Fullerton Flying Services did the following work to make N7826C airworthy: "Recovered two flaps, two ailerons, two elevators and the rudder. Ceconite fabric used." Sold on January 27, 1964, to used aircraft dealer T. A.

C/n D.1073, BuNo 121699, F8F-2, N7826C, at Concord, California, after a ferry flight from NAS North Island in October 1958. Note its faded Jacksonville Reserve squadron markings spray-painted over and its new civil identity sprayed on. Parked behind is N7827C. (William T. Larkins)

Underwood of Phoenix, AZ, for $6,000.00 and 521 hours TT. Sold by Underwood to William Fuller and Shelby Kritser of Fort Worth, TX, for $1.00 and OVC[35] for the purpose of "exhibition" with a TT of 523.5 hours on March 28, 1964. A permit of "Amended Experimental Operations Restrictions" was issued on July 7, 1966, at the request of Kritser, stating "Exhibition flights are authorized for pilot proficiency, for exhibition, and for travel to and from exhibition areas. Flight tests are permitted in accordance with FAR 91" with an expiration date of July 7, 1967. On August 13, 1966, N7826C was written off in a fatal accident while flown by Kritser at Amarillo Air Force Base, TX, during an aerobatic routine. The FAA cancelled the registration at Fuller's request on July 14, 1970.

---

34  One of three that Acme bought that day, all for the same price. The other two were c/n D.1126 and c/n D.1227

35  OVC is a frequently used term in the sale of high-value items, such as aircraft and cars, to avoid paying high sales tax

C/n D.1073, N7826C, now back in southern California at Orange County Airport in December 1962. It was photographed near the Tallmantz Air Museum, but was not part of the museum. The only real change was the proper stenciling of its registration number. (Emil Strasser)

C/n D.1073, N7826C, at the Van Nuys, California, airport in 1964 after being stripped. The aircraft is bare metal and was owned by aircraft dealer T. A. Underwood. It would be sold to Kritser and Fuller within weeks of this photo being taken. (Jerry Liang)

C/n D.1073, N7826C, being refueled at Fort Worth, Texas, in 1965. It appears to be very clean. (Jay Miller Collection)

# C/N D.1081

BuNo 121707 F8F-2
Acceptance date: August 19, 1948
Delivery date: In delivery to NAS San Diego, CA, in August 1948

To Pool NAS San Diego in September 1948. To Pool NAS Alameda, CA, in October 1948. Minor landing accident while assigned to Composite Squadron Fifty, VC-50, on April 19, 1949. To O&R NAS Alameda in October 1949. Stricken. Sold as surplus May 27, 1958, to Stinson Field Aircraft[36] of San Antonio, TX, and not registered until April 28, 1960, as N1027B. Sold in 1962 to Kaman Aircraft Corp of Bloomfield, CT. The registration number was kept for record purposes until cancelled on May 18, 1965. After ferry flight to Connecticut, the Bearcat was anchored next to runways for use as a wind generator with its outer wing panels removed and not flown again. Ownership transferred to Defense Contract Administrative Services Office (DCAS) in Bloomfield, CT. DCAS transferred N1027B ownership to Marine Corps Aviation Museum in Quantico, VA, on September 16, 1970, where it went into storage disassembled. Moved to Mojave, CA, disassembled by April 1978 for restoration for USMC by McDonnell Enterprises and Wally McDonnell. Sold or traded to Wally McDonnell of Mojave on April 16, 1980. Sold in 1982 to Elmer Ward of Santa Ana, CA, for restoration to flying. In 1992, Ward applied to the FAA for registration number NL3025 for an airframe to carry c/n D.739A with intentions of using a major part of N1027B and N7701C. In addition, new manufactured parts would be used to recreate NL3025, the original G-58A that had been written off in 1949. During the restoration, the airframe was converted to a two-seater with a longer canopy and space for a passenger behind the pilot by removing the rollover structure. The aircraft was first flown on July 27,1992, as NL3025, c/n D.739A. The Bearcat was painted in the colors of Maj. Al Williams' *Gulfhawk 4th* and flown by Ward around the country at airshows. This Bearcat was heavily damaged at Oshkosh, WI, on August 1, 1993.

C/n D.1081, BuNo 121707, F8F-2, N1027B, components after arrival at the Mojave, California, airport in April 1978 from the United States Marine Corps Museum. It was 80 percent complete when it arrived at the museum from Kaman. (Bob Kennedy)

Ward was slightly injured and the aircraft remains were trucked back to Chino, CA. The ownership transferred to Steve Hinton, John Hinton, John Maloney and Kevin Eldridge of Chino around 2005. During the slow restoration to flying, the Bearcat was restored to a single seater. First flight was May 8, 2020, as NL3025 and registered to Steve Hinton. It is currently flying in United States Navy overall blue paint scheme.

---

36  One of five Stinson Field Aircraft bought that day. The company had already bought two the day before, for a total of seven

C/n D.1081, N1027B; the aft fuselage, windshield and, at right, the wing stub and center section in Wally McDonnell's Mojave, California, hangar in April 1978. (Bob Kennedy)

C/n D.1081, now transformed into c/n D.739A, NL3025 (#2), rebuilt to represent the original *Gulfhawk 4th*. Photographed at Madera, California, in August 1992, shortly after D.739A made its first flight since flying into Kaman Helicopter facility in Bloomington, Connecticut, in 1962. Note the elongated canopy to accommodate a passenger. (Bob Kennedy)

C/n D.1081 (as c/n D.739A), NL3025, inflight showing the fine detail and workmanship performed by Elmer Ward. (Jim Dunn)

C/n D.1081, NL3025 (#2), shortly after an accident at Oshkosh, Wisconsin, in August 1993. The Bearcat cartwheeled at least once before coming to rest. The fuselage was broken just aft of the canopy and both wings were heavily damaged. (Nicholas A. Veronico)

C/n D.1081, NL3025, made its first flight in May 2020 following a long rebuild after it had been converted back to a single-seater. V-56 is carried as a tribute to the first F8F owned by the Planes of Fame Air Museum in the 1960s. Steve Hinton and crew did amazing work. Photo taken in 2021. (Jim Dunn)

# C/N D.1088

BuNo 121714, F8F-2P
Acceptance date: August 27,1948
Delivery date: In delivery, not legible

To Pool NAS Pensacola, FL.To Pool NAS Alameda, CA, in November 1948. No other information on History Card. Donated on November 25, 1958, to "The Air Museum" as surplus equipment from NAS North Island, CA. Registered N4995V to Edward T. Maloney and The Air Museum of Claremont, CA, on the same date. Reported as having 1,174.1 hours TT on August 4, 1962. Sold on August 25, 1972, to B&S Advertising of Knoxville, Tennessee (TN), and re-registered as N1YY. B&S Advertising was owned by Harold "Bubba" Beal and Charles "Chub" Smith[37]. When B&S purchased the F8F from the museum, the Bearcat had only flown 29 hours in 14 years and had its original R-2800-30W with its AEC still installed. It was completely overhauled in 1975 and registration changed to N700H. Bearcat was reported to have been flown weekly while with B&S as it had accumulated 1,480.3 hours TT by June 4, 1980. Sold on November 19, 1980, to Patina Ltd, (The Fighter Collection/Stephen Grey) of Geneva, Switzerland, and the registration changed to N700HL. Bearcat was flown throughout the UK and Europe from 1981 to 1998, still registered as N700HL. Registration changed at owners' request to G-RUMM on March 16, 1998. Currently flying with The Fighter Collection.

---

37 Beal and Smith would own/co-own five Bearcats between them through the years

C/n D.1088, BuNo 121714, F8F-2, N4995V, just after arriving at Ontario Airport, California, from NAS North Island in 1959. It had been donated to the Planes of Fame Air Museum by the Navy. Bearcat N4995V retained its military markings while owned and flown by the museum. (Albert Hansen)

C/n D.1088, N4995V, in June 1972, at Chino airport after the Planes of Fame Air Museum moved there from Ontario, California; the aircraft is still wearing pseudo-military markings. Bearcat N4995V was owned by the museum from 1959 until sold to B&S Advertising in 1977. (John Stewart)

C/n D.1088 now registered as NX700H, and carrying the markings of VF-11 "The Red Rippers" at Roanoke, Virginia, in May 1979, while owned by B&S Advertising. B&S was associated with five Bearcats. (Jim Sullivan)

*Left*: C/n D.1088 after it was sold across the Atlantic to Steven Gray as N700HL. Based in England since 1981, 121714 is a regular performer at European airshows. (A.J. Clarke via Dick Phillips)

*Opposite*: C/n D.1088 as it looks today and registered as G-RUMM at Duxford Air Base. It is flown regularly and well maintained by the fighter collection. (Dick Phillips Collection)

# C/N D.1105

BuNo 121731 F8F-2
Acceptance date: September 17,1948
Delivery date: In delivery September 1948

To Pool NAS San Diego, CA, in October 1948. To Pool NAS Alameda, CA, in November 1948. Stricken date not noted. Sold as surplus on May 27, 1958, to Stinson Field Aircraft[38] of San Antonio, TX, for $708.91 and registered as N1028B. Sold on August 15, 1958, to Transair Inc of Linden, NJ, for $10.00 OVC. Sold on November 30, 1961, to New Jersey Air Co of Hackensack, NJ, for $1.00 OVC, along with N1029B. The company began to modify them for aerial survey work. Sold on November 1, 1963, to SkyService Inc of Linden for $420.00 via a mechanic's lien by order of the State of New Jersey. Sold to Norwood R. Hanson and Chester F. Christopher of New Shrewsbury, NJ, on January 16, 1964, for $1.00 average order value (AOV) for use in "exhibition flying" with 870.9 hours TT. Registration was changed to N500B on March 18, 1964, at the request of Christopher and Hanson, who owned N5555H. They flew a dual Bearcat aerobatics routine. On April 23, 1966, Hanson sold his half of N500B to Christopher for $1.00 AOV. In January 1968, Christopher changed the registration number to N5005 and asked the FAA to hold N500B for future use.

C/n D.1105, BuNo 121731, F8F-2, N500B, at an airshow in the Midwest in the early 1960s. The Bearcat was flown by Chester Christopher. He and Norwood Hanson co-owned this Bearcat and flew a dual Bearcat aerobatic routine before Hanson was fatally injured in his Bearcat. (Dave Ostrowski via David W. Menard)

Sold on April 26, 1968, to Judson Smith of Lebanon, NJ, for $1.00 AOV on the FAA Bill of Sale. In reality, the loan was financed by a New Jersey bank for $31,279.20; this was one year after Hanson had been killed in the crash of N5555H. Sold on November 18, 1969, to Michael A. Geren of Kansas City, MO, with 959.2 hours TT for $1.00 OVC on the FAA Bill of Sale. It had only flown 88.3 hours during the previous five years. Geren and his partner Ron E. Reynolds applied for an "Experimental Certification[39]" on June 4, 1971, for the purpose of racing and exhibition" with 986.54 hours TT and 27.25 hours flown since it had been purchased. Geren and Reynolds raced N5005 several times, as Race #44 at Reno in September 1970 and at the Mojave 1000 in November 1970 as Race #66. The following year they entered it in the July 1971 U.S. Cup Race as Race #44 at San Diego, CA. It was during this race that N5005 developed an engine fire and crashed fatally injuring Geren on July 18, 1971. The FAA cancelled the registration on September 10, 1971.

---

38  One of five Stinson Field Aircraft bought on this date

39  For operating limitations, see Chapter Six

C/n D.1105, now N5005, and wholly owned by Chester Christopher. He had the registration number changed in 1968 after he bought Hanson's half of the Bearcat in 1966. (Dick Phillips Collection)

C/n D.1105, Race #44, at Reno in September 1970. The race number is barely visible due to exhaust stains down the side. Ron Reynolds flew #44 at 349.7mph to qualify 11th and would place second in the Silver race that year. (Jerry Liang)

C/n D.1105, Race #44, being taxied out by Mike Geren at the 1971 United States Cup Race at San Diego, California. Geren and Reynolds shared racing duties during the 100-lap, 1,000-mile race during which Geren was fatally injured. (Jerry Liang)

# C/N D.1122

BuNo 121748 F8F-2

Acceptance date: September 29, 1948

Delivery date: In delivery September 1948

To Pool NAS Alameda, CA, in October 1948. Assigned to NAS Norfolk Reserve Squadron sometime before being withdrawn from service. Stricken date unknown. Sold as surplus on May 27, 1958, to Stinson Field Aircraft of San Antonio, TX, for $658.91 and registered as N1029B. Sold on August 27, 1958, to Transair Inc of Linden, NJ. Sold on November 30, 1961, to New Jersey Air Co of Hackensack, NJ, which began to modify it for aerial survey work. Sold on November 1, 1963, to SkyService Inc of Linden for $420.00 via a mechanic's lien by the State of New Jersey. Sold on December 15, 1963, to Michael E. Coutches of Fremont, CA. Sold on June 1, 1965, to John Church[40] of Alameda, CA, and reregistered as N618F on August 18, 1965. Sold January 8, 1966, to Stanley Kurzet of Covina, CA, and reported as having 582.1 hours TT. Sold on March 3, 1971, to Travis T. Morris of Van Nuys, CA, with 584.4 hours TT. Morris raced in the California 1000 at Mojave in November 1971 as Race #7. The Bearcat had a Lockheed P2V spinner added and a P-51H propellor and finished ninth overall. However, the sale to Morris was disputed and claims filed to void the sale. After a lengthy court fight, the title returned to Kurzet on November 5, 1973.

C/n D.1122, BuNo 121748, F8F-2, photographed on July 12, 1958, just after being acquired by New Jersey Air Service. It was registered N1029B and wore its markings from the time it served with the Reserve Squadron at NAS Norfolk, Virginia. (Charles N. Trask via William T. Larkins)

Sold on December 22, 1973, to John B. Gury III[41] of St. Louis, MO, and registration changed to N200N. Sold by order of the court in November 1976 to Mary J. Gury of St. Louis, due to the death of John. Sold on August 27, 1979, to B&S Advertising of Knoxville, TN, for $85,000.00 and reported as having 590.5 hours TT, having only flown 6.1 hours in six years. Sold on December 31, 1979, to World Jet Inc of Fort Lauderdale, FL, (Whittington Brothers Inc) and ferried to Fort Collins, CO, where the Bearcat was placed in storage. FAA records continued to show B&S as the registered owner until 1997 (sale reported on card). Sold on October 17, 1997, to Thomas Springer, no reported address. Sold the same day to Sonoma Valley Aircraft Inc (George Perez) of Petaluma, CA. The Bearcat was ferried to Santa Rosa, CA, then to Ione, CA, in 1998 for rebuild work. It still had its original R-2800-30W and AEC installed. Sold in September 1999 to Air B Aviation (Rene Bouverat) of Marnaz, France) and registered as F-AZRJ and given French Armee de l' Air markings. The first flight after rebuilding was on September 28, 1999. It was de-registered on December 7, 1999, and shipped to France. Returned to the United States in 2005 and sold to Ray Dieckman of Chino, CA, and registered as N224RD and repainted in United States Navy markings. Dieckman raced it at Reno in 2007 as Race #224 and placed third in the Silver final race. Sold on November 27, 2007, to Comanche Warbirds (Dan Friedkin) of Houston, TX, and registered as N1DF and is currently flying.

---

40  One of three John Church owned over the years

41  John B. Gury III bought this second Bearcat as he already owned c/n D.1190

C/n D.1122, now as N618F, on the ramp at Reno in September 1966. It was flown in for display by aircraft dealer Stanley Kurzet. The Reno races have always been a great place to display aircraft for sale. Bearcat N618F did not qualify or race. (Peter B. Lewis)

C/n D.1122 as Race #7 at the 1971 California 1000 Air Race at Mojave, where it was flown by its owner Travis Morris. He finished ninth overall. (Jerry Liang)

C/n D.1122 at Fort Collins, Colorado, and registered as N200N before being sold to World Jet by B&S Advertising. *The Red Ship* would remain out of sight for almost 16 years until sold again in 1998. (Harold F. Beal)

C/n D.1122 in October 1999 at Ione, California, after overhaul and repainting in Armee de l'Air markings. The Bearcat carried dual registration numbers N200N and F-AZRJ, the latter of which is its new French registration. When received for overhaul, it still had its original -30W engine. (Jim Dunn)

C/n D.1122, F-AZRJ, at Duxford Air Base, England, in July 2002. While in Europe it flew at numerous airshows before returning to the United States in 2005. (John Kerr)

C/n D.1122, now as N224RD, at the 2007 Reno Air Races, flown by owner Ray Dieckman as Race #224. Dieckman placed third in the Silver race. (Jerry Liang)

C/n D.1122 at Chino, California, in May 2009, registered as NX1DF. It was owned by Dan and Tom Friedkin who bought the Bearcat in 2007. Currently with Dan and Tom Friedkin's Comanche Fighters. (Jerry Liang)

# C/N D.1125

BuNo 121751 F8F-2
Acceptance date: September 30, 1948
Delivery date: In delivery September 1948

To Pool at NAS Alameda, CA, in October 1948. No further information on History Card. Stricken date unknown. Sold as surplus on July 31, 1958, to Texas Aviation Material Inc[42] of Dallas, TX, for $449.64 and registered as N9885C. Sold on October 8, 1958, to Daniel F. Neuman of St. Paul, MN, for $1.00 OVC. Sold on January 5, 1959, to D. A. Hackett of Phoenix, AZ, for $1,200.00. Sold on January 12, 1959, to William "Bill" Stead[43] of Reno, NV, for $1.00 OVC. It appears that N9885C had not been flown or civilianized by its previous owners as the first Application for Airworthiness was not filed with the FAA until February 22, 1960, by Stead. At that time, N9885C was reported to have 603.9 hours TT and 165.0 hours since major overhaul (SMOH) by the United States Navy. During the time it was owned by Stead it was flown by Mira Slovak. It won the inaugural 1964 National Air Races at Sky Ranch, NV, as Race #80. It was also raced at Boulder City, NV, and Lancaster, CA. After the death of Bill Stead in May 1966, the Bearcat was sold on July 12, 1966, to Moseley Aviation Inc of Tolleson, AZ, with 702 hours TT. Sold again on November 22, 1968, to I. N. "Junior" Burchinal of Brookston, TX, with 715.2 hours TT. The Bearcat was used in Burchinal's "Fighter School" to teach pilots to fly warbirds. Sold on November 14, 1972, to Mike Smith of Johnson, Kansas (KS). Smith raced it from 1973 to 1975 as Race #41 *Lois Jean* at Reno and Mojave, CA, with mixed results. Sold on June 1, 1976, to Roy N. Lotspeich Publishing Co of Knoxville, TN, (Charles H. "Chub" Smith) with 833.5 hours TT and 233 hours since purchased by Bill Stead in 1960. Bearcat N9885C was written off in a fatal accident flown by Smith on June 18, 1980. On its last annual inspection, N9885C had accumulated 974.3hours TT. It was de-registered on October 15, 1981, by the FAA as having been totally destroyed.

C/n D.1125, BuNo 121751, F8F-2, N9885C, at the Los Angeles National Air Races held in Lancaster, California, in 1965. It was flown by Mira Slovak. Race #80 competed in 1964 and 1965, while owned by William "Bill" Stead who was one of the originators of the Reno Air Races. (Emil Strasser)

---

42  This is one of two Bearcats Texas Aviation Material bought this day. The other was c/n D.902, for which they paid the same price

43  Bill Stead was one of the originators of modern Unlimited Air Racing in 1964

C/n D.1125 competed as Race #41 by owner Mike Smith at Reno in 1973 in a pseudo-military paint scheme. (William T. Larkins)

C/n D.1125, Race #41, N9885C, was towed back to the pits at Reno in 1973 carrying the name *Lois Jean*. Smith would also race #41 in the 1973 Mojave races. (Jerry Liang)

C/n D.1125 at the 1978 Oshkosh airshow. Bearcat N9885C was in the markings of VF-11 "Red Rippers." It was owned by Charles "Chub" Smith, who flew it on a regular basis. (John Kerr)

C/n D.1125, N9885C, at Roanoke, Virginia, in May 1979, with Harold Beal's N800H in the background. Smith and Beal flew together and co-owned several Bearcats until Smith's fatal accident in June 1980. Bearcat N9885C had flown about 371 hours total time since it was surplused at Naval Air Station North Island in 1958. (Jim Sullivan)

# C/N D.1126

BuNo 121752 F8F-2
Acceptance date: September 30, 1948
Delivery date: In delivery September 1948 to Pool
at NAS Alameda, CA

No other information on History Card. Stricken date unknown. Sold as surplus on August 15, 1958, to Acme Aircraft Parts Inc, (Louis Walter/ Roger Keeney) of Compton, CA, for $611.99. Sold on August 20, 1958, to John W. and Mary W. Dorr[44] of Orinda, CA, for $1,100.00 and registered as N7827C. A K-24 aerial camera was installed by Roger Keeney. On December 9, 1959, the Bearcat was reported to have 660.8 hours TT. Sold on April 18, 1964, to Thomas P. Mathews of Monterey, CA, who used it for air racing as Race #10. The aircraft first raced at Reno in 1964 flown by Walt Ohlrich and at other races for Mathews until 1966. Sold to Walter E. Ohlrich of Tulsa, OK, on November 8, 1967. Ohlrich raced it until he sold it on November 13, 1971, to John A. Herlihy of Moss Beach, CA, for $5,000.00. Herlihy raced it as #8 until 1973. In September 1973 Herlihy traded N7827C to Harold F. Beal III of Knoxville, TN, for Beal's P-51D NL11T. On January 10, 1974, Beal changed the registration to number N2YY and the registered owner became B&S Advertising Co of Knoxville, TN. In 1975, B&S changed the registration number N800H. B&S sold N800H on August 25, 1977, to Whittington Brothers (Bill and Don) Inc of West Palm Beach, FL. The brothers raced it as Race #8 throughout the early 1980s. The Bearcat was reported to have 1,078.35 hours TT by September 1977. Sold on September 8, 1990, to Douglas Arnold of Switzerland (Warbirds of Great Britain) and arrived in England in December 1990. The Bearcat remained registered to Whittington's until 1994. This Bearcat rarely flew while in England

C/n D.1126, BuNo 121752, F8F-2, at Concord, California, with its newly spray painted registration number N7827C on October 4, 1958. It was flown on a ferry permit from NAS North Island to Concord for its new owners John and Mary Dorr. It should be noted that N7827C was first assigned to the Pool and NAS Alameda just across the Bay. (William T. Larkins)

and was in storage. Sold to Iron Baron Corp, J. C. Ellis director, of Dover, DE. Sold on April 9, 1998, to Patina Ltd, Steven Grey's "Fighter Collection." Sold same day to Corporate Aircraft Inc of Fresno, CA. Sold on April 10, 1998, to Talon Investment LLC of Eugene, OR. It competed at Reno in September as Race #106 flown by former astronaut William "Bill" A. Anders. He raced it again at Reno in 1999. Sold on March 30, 1999, to Heritage Flight Museum, of which Bill Anders was a founder, in Eastsound, WA. Bearcat N800H was damaged in a landing accident at Stockton, CA, on September 26, 1999. Sold to John Sessions Historic Aircraft Foundation of Seattle, WA, on September 7, 2006. Titled owner changed to P-40 Kittyhawk LLC on September 4, 2022. With the Erickson Aircraft Collection in Madras, OR, since April 2022 and is regularly flown.

---

44  John and Mary Dorr bought two that day from Acme. The other was c/n D.1073

C/n D.1126, N7827C, competed at the 1966 Reno Air Races and was flown by Sandy Falconer for owner Tom Mathews. Race #10 was one of three F8Fs that qualified that year and placed third in the Consolation race. (William T. Larkins)

C/n D.1126, N7827C, shown on the ramp at Oakland, California. It sports both *Tonopah Miss* on the cowling and *Tomcat* just below the windscreen. This would be around the time Mathews sold Race #10 to Commander (Ret.) Walt Ohlrich. The Bearcat's color is Navy blue. (John Kerr)

C/n D.1126 as Race #10 in a new paint scheme and named *Miss Priss* competed at the 1969 Reno Air Races. Walt Ohlrich earned a first place in the Consolation Race and collected $2,000 prize money. (Jerry Liang)

C/n D.1126 as Race #8 at Reno in 1972, flown by its new owner John Herlihy and named *Sweet P*. Herlihy qualified 14th out of 16 and would finish fourth in the Silver race. (William T. Larkins)

By the time of the 1973 Reno races, Herlihy had stripped the paint off c/n D.1126, N7827C, in preparation for repainting. He traded D.1126 for a P-51 Mustang before that happened. (Jerry Liang)

C/n D.1126, wearing its short-lived registration number N2YY, just after emerging from a complete overhaul at Chino, California, in August 1975. Its new owner, Harold F. Beal, changed the registration again to N800H. (Albert Hansen)

C/n D.1126, NX800H, now owned by Bill and Don Whittington, competed as Race #8 at the 1980 Reno Air Races. (William T. Larkins)

C/n D.1126, NX800H, remained with the Whittingtons from 1978–90 with rare outings at Reno until sold to Warbirds of Great Britain in December 1990. Race #8 *Bearcat Bill* is at Reno in 1981. (Jerry Liang)

C/n D.1126, NX800H, after it was repainted in miliary markings. While with the Warbirds of Great Britain, it was rarely seen or flown. When photographed in 1996, it had already been sold back across the Atlantic. (A. J. Clarke)

C/n D.1126, NX800H, at the Reno Air Races in September 1999 and owned by former NASA astronaut William Anders. It competed as Race #106 *Wampus Cat*. (Bob Kennedy)

C/n D.1126, N800H, has been flying with the Erickson Aircraft Collection of Madras, Oregon, since April 2022. (Erickson Aircraft Collection)

# C/N D.1148

BuNo 122619 F8F-2
Acceptance date: October 29,1948
Delivery date: In delivery October 1948

To Pool NAS Alameda, CA, in November 1948. No other information on History Card. Stricken date unknown. To storage at NAS North Island, CA, with less than 300 hours TT on the engine. Sold as surplus on August 1, 1958, to John M. Wells of Mercedes, TX, for $855.00 and registered as N7958C. Sold on February 1, 1959, to Bearcat and Co (John M. Wells co-owner) of Rio Hondo, TX, and reported as having 616.2hours TT. Sold on May 22, 1961, to B. Frank Williams of Port Arthur, TX, for $3,800.00. Sold on March 6, 1963, to T. A. Underwood[45] of Buckeye, AZ. Sold on May 5, 1963, to Naylor Aviation of California Inc in Oakland, CA. Sold April 13, 1963, on consignment to Larry Hamilton dba Hamilton Aircraft of Sonoma, CA, for $6,000.00. Repossessed April 6, 1964, by Appliance Buyers Credit Corp of St. Louis, MI, the registered owner. Sold on September 24, 1964, to Gardner Flyers Inc of Brownwood, TX, Marvin L. "Lefty" Gardner president. Sold on April 9, 1965, to Aviation Amazement-Amusement Inc of Oklahoma City, OK, Marvin Gardner president. Sold on November 1, 1967, to Gardner Flyers Inc. It is during this time that this Bearcat is associated with the Confederate Air

C/n D.1148, BuNo 122619, F8F-2, N7958C, at Chino, California, in 1973. Bearcat N7958C was sold from NAS North Island for $855.00 in 1958 and went through numerous owners by 1973. This Bearcat is one of three associated with the Confederate Air Force in the 1960s. (Jerry Liang)

Force, though that organisation's name was never on the Bill of Sale. Sold on December 27, 1971, to Kenneth D. Boomhower and Max R. Hoffman of Hays, KS, for $30,000.00. Sold on May 15, 1973, to B&S Advertising. Sold on January 10, 1974, to Harold F. Beal III. The registration number was changed to N700F on March 20, 1974, by Beal. Sold on August 18, 1978, to World Jet Inc, (Whittington Brothers), of Fort Lauderdale, FL, and registration changed to N14WB. Bearcat was reported to have 678.5 hours TT. Sold or loaned on September 15, 1983, to Experimental Aircraft Association (EAA) of Oshkosh, WI, and placed on display. Sold on September 1, 1994, to Yesterday Museum Inc at the same address as World Jet in Fort Lauderdale. Bearcat N14WB was flown out

of Oshkosh in late 1998 to an unknown location and eventually to Fort Lauderdale where it was registered to World Jet on September 2, 1999. Sold on June 18, 2002, to Ron Buccarelli, Lake Air Inc, of Fort Lauderdale. To consignment/sale to Provenance Fighters of California in 2007. It was raced at Reno in September 2007 by Dave Morss as Race #23 and placed eighth in the Silver race. To Rod Lewis/Lewis Fighter Fleet of San Antonio, TX, on January 1, 2008. Current with Spitfire Ventures LLC at the same address. This Bearcat is called the "Chrome Cat" because, during its overhaul in the 1980s, just about everything that could be chrome plated was; landing gear and interior doors, engine parts, roll-over structure, and tailwheel. It flies regularly.

---

45 T.A. Underwood ran a crop-dusting service and also bought and sold surplus military aircraft, mainly warbirds

C/n D.1148 as it emerged from rebuild as N700F at Chino, California, in 1975 and before painting. Bearcat N700F was eventually painted in Naval Reserve markings by B&S Advertising (Harold Beal). B&S kept it for five years. (Bob Kennedy)

C/n D.1148 now registered as N14WB to World Jet Inc, making a stop at Denver, Colorado, in 1981. Shortly afterward it was loaned to the Experimental Aircraft Association (EAA) Museum in Oshkosh, Wisconsin. (John Stewart)

C/n D.1148, N14WB, as seen after its sale to Rod Lewis of Lewis Fighter Fleet in San Antonio, Texas. The photo shows why it is called the *Chrome Cat*. Its Denver Reserve Squadron markings make it one of the best-looking Bearcats. (Jay Miller)

C/n D.1148, N14WB, had several owners and competed at Reno as Race #23. The *Chrome Cat* was sold to Rod Lewis of Lewis Fighter Fleet in September 2008. It flies regularly as of 2024. (Jay Miller)

# C/N D.1162

BuNo 121776 F8F-2
Acceptance date: November 18, 1948
Delivery date: Not legible

Delivered to Pool location and date not legible, then to VF-113 with CVG-11 at NAS San Diego, CA, in March 1950. To FASRON 11 at NAS San Diego in March 1950 with 324 hours TT airframe. To FASRON 8 at NAS Alameda, CA, in June 1950. To O&R, BuAer M&S at NAS Alameda on October 13, 1950, with 330 hours TT. To O&R BuAer M&S NAS Norfolk, VA, on August 13, 1951. To Marine Training Squadron One, VMT-1, at MCAS Cherry Point, NC, on August 24, 1951. To Marine Fighter Training Squadron Twenty, VMFT-20, at MCAS Cherry Point on January 23, 1952. VMFT-20 reported 562 hours TT in August 1952. To NART Birmingham, AL, on September 12, 1952. To O&R BuAer M&S NAS Corpus Christi, TX, on January 3, 1953. Returned to NART Birmingham on February 11, 1953, with 585 hours TT. To O&R BuAer M&S NAS San Diego, on May 17, 1953, with 606 hours TT. To O&R BuAer FA at NAS San Diego on February 29, 1956, with 606 hours TT. Stricken from inventory on January 9, 1957. Sold as surplus on May 27, 1958, to Stinson Field Aircraft[46] of San Antonio, TX, for $658.91 and registered as N1030B. Sold

C/n D.1162, BuNo 121776, F8F-2, N0130B, in storage at the Marine Corps Museum, Quantico, Virginia, in 1989. This Bearcat had been used by Kaman Aircraft as a wind machine until donated to the museum in the 1970s. (Charles Ritchey)

on August 28, 1958, to Transair Inc of Linden, NJ. Sold on December 30, 1959, to Kaman Aircraft Corp of Bloomfield, CT, not civilianized and price undisclosed. Flown from Linden to Bloomfield. Registration number N1030B kept for record keeping until May 1965 when Kaman cancelled as aircraft "has been permanently retired from service." After delivery to Kaman, the Bearcat had its outer wing panels removed and was anchored next to the runways for use as a wind generator and not flown again. Ownership transferred to Defense Contract Administrative Services Office (DCAS) of Bloomfield, CT. DCAS transferred N1030B ownership to Marine Corps Aviation Museum, MCAS Quantico, VA, on September 16, 1970. Moved to storage, partly disassembled. Sold or traded in June 1996 to Lone Star Flight Museum, (Robert L. Waltrip) of Galveston, TX, and registered as N68RW for restoration to flight status. Trucked to Galveston to begin restoration, then to Milton, FL, where it made its first flight in 44 years in March 2003. On display at museum and rarely flown until sold on May 23, 2011, to John O' Connor/BA1945 LLC. It qualified to race at Reno in September 2011 as Race #52 by Nelson Ezell, but did not race. In August 2020, it was shipped via the aircraft carrier USS *Essex* to Hawaii for a commemoration celebration. It was slightly damaged in a taxiing accident at Wheeler AFB. It was shipped back to the mainland and repaired. Currently flying and is for sale.

---

46  One of four Stinson Field Aircraft bought that day

C/n D.1162 in spite of being outdoors for more than 15 years, N1030B was in good shape when sold to the Lone Star Flight Museum. It retained its original markings. (Charles Ritchey)

C/n D.1162 was rebuilt in Milton, Florida, in April 2002. The registration was changed in 1996 to N68RW by Robert Waltrip. (John Kerr)

C/n D.1162 N68RW seen in March 2003, painted as *Blue Angels #1* after its first flight in 44 years. It was rarely flown after that. (Jim G. Firmin)

C/n D.1162 N68RW was shipped to Hawaii aboard the USS *Essex* in August 2020 for a commemoration celebration. The Bearcat suffered minor damage there in a taxiing accident, but was repaired. Currently flying and for sale as of 2024. (Jim G. Firmin)

# C/N D.1171

BuNo 122629 F8F-2
Acceptance date: November 30,1948
Delivery date: In delivery November 1948 to Pool

To VF-91 at NAS Quonset Point, RI, in May 1950 with 388 hours TT. To VF-34 of CVG-3 at NAS Quonset Point in June 1950. To O&R BuAer M&S at NAS Norfolk, VA, on September 18, 1950. To NARTU NAS Norfolk on December 29, 1951. To FASRON 5 at NAS Oceana, VA, on February 2, 1952. To VF-752 at NAS Oceana on June 4, 1952, with 558 hours TT. To NART Birmingham, AL, on September 8, 1952, with 563 hours TT. To O&R BuAer M&S at NAS Corpus Christi, TX, on December 30, 1953, with 653 hours TT. To O&R BuAer M&S NAS San Diego, CA, on October 22, 1954. To O&R BuAer FA NAS San Diego on August 31, 1955. Retirement O&R BuAer FA San Diego on February 29, 1956. Stricken from inventory on January 9, 1957, with 667 hours TT. Sold at NAS North Island on May 26, 1958, to Stinson Field Aircraft[47] of San Antonio for $788.91 and registered as N1031B. Sold on August 27, 1958, to Treadwell Aviation Corp of Coconut Grove, FL. Sold on November 6, 1959, to Alexander E. Stoddard of Dade City, FL. Sold on May 10, 1960, to Salvatore Martino of Bradenton, FL, for "aerial photography." The rumor is that this sale may have

C/n D.1171, BuNo 122629, F8F-2, N1031B, at Valparaíso, Indiana, in 1962 after a landing accident when it cartwheeled off the side of the runway. N1031B was further damaged when it was dragged back to the airport. (Chuck Adams via Lyle Shelton)

been connected to the invasion of Cuba, but nothing has ever been confirmed. Sold on November 18, 1961, to Florida Airmotive Sales of Ft. Lauderdale with 671.1 hours TT, having only flown 4.1 hours since being sold by the Navy. Sold on December 18, 1961, to William R. Eckhart, address unknown, for $4,804.90. Sold on July 25, 1962, to Tim O'Neill of Lake Geneva, WI. Crashed on landing and overturned at Valparaiso, IN, while on its delivery flight August 21, 1962. Pilot Richard Fennell was slightly injured and the Bearcat heavily damaged. Its remains were dragged back to the airport and abandoned. Registration canceled at owner's request February 4, 1963, as dismantled or salvaged. Remains sold to Earl Reinert[48] Wheeling, IL, in January 1963. Remains sold to Michael Coutches of American Aircraft Sales in October 1966 for $4,000.00. Remains were kept at Valparaiso until sold on May 10, 1968, to Lyle Shelton for $2,500.00. What he obtained were the inboard wings/center section and aft fuselage, the remainder had been stripped over the years. Using pieces from other wrecks, some from N212KA, and a Wright R-3350 engine, Shelton was able to assemble a flyable aircraft for racing that he registered in the "Experimental" category as N777L. The former Navy fighter pilot continued to progressively modify and tweak it to become a world speed record holder and one of the all-time winners of Unlimited air racing. First raced as Race #70 and then as #77, it has raced at most of the Unlimited race venues and has garnered 16 Gold wins in spite of two accidents and many blown engines. Bearcat N777L competed in its last race at Reno 2015. It was on display at Reno 2016–17. Sold at the end of 2006 to Rod Lewis along with the racing team name. Currently with the Air Legends Foundation (Rod Lewis), in storage, and undergoing preservation/restoration.

---

47  One of two bought that day. The other was c/n D.1201

48  Earl Reinert was an early warbird collector while Michael Coutches was an aircraft broker/salesman

C/n D.1171 another view of N1031B at Valparaiso, Indiana, shortly after the accident. The pilot was uninjured and N1031B does not appear too badly damaged. The remains were left at Valparaiso until Lyle Shelton purchased them in 1968. By that time, they had been picked over and Shelton did not receive a complete aircraft. (Chuck Adams via Lyle Shelton)

The elements of D.1171 that Shelton retrieved. (Hal Loomis Collection)

C/n D.1171, now N777L as Race #70, arriving at the Reno Air Races in September 1969. This was 14 months after it was first purchased as a wreck by Lyle Shelton. It now had a Wright R-3350-26WA engine and a DC-7 prop and spinner. (Emil Strasser)

C/n D.1171 at Reno 1969 painted in zinc-chromate yellow and ready to race. Race #70 finished fifth in the Gold race. When trucked to Los Angeles, California, in June 1968, it had no engine, outer wing panels, prop, or canopy, and the vertical tail had been crushed. (William T. Larkins)

C/n D.1171, N777L, as Race #77 at Cape May, New Jersey, in June 1971 where it would score its first win. (Dick Phillips Collection)

C/n D.1171 at Reno in September 1970. *Able Cat* would qualify fifth at 373.46mph and DNF in the Gold race after major engine trouble. Lyle Shelton was forced to ground loop #77 after blowing both tires on landing, but the aircraft suffered only minor damage. (Emil Strasser)

C/n D.1171 with long-range ferry tanks and cut-down canopy at San Diego, California, for the California 1000 Race in July 1971, where it finished fourth overall. It was at this event that Mike Geren was fatally injured in the crash of Race #44. (Jerry Liang)

C/n D.1171 at Reno in September 1972 as *Phast Phoenix,* wearing Purple People Eater colors. Lyle Shelton qualified third and finished second in the Gold race. Note the standard windscreen, canopy and patch on the tail. During a flight to test a new shorter wing, the canopy blew off, causing damage. Shelton was able to borrow a replacement canopy and continued to race. (Emil Strasser)

C/n D.1171, N777L, taxiing back to the pit area in 1974 with a jubilant Lyle Shelton waving to the crowd believing he had just won the Reno Championship race with a new race record of 431.61mph. However, #77 was bumped to fifth place by the judges for not pulling up during the two maydays called during the race. (Bill LeSanche)

C/n D.1171, N777L on the line at the 1974 Mojave race where Lyle Shelton was the top qualifier and took second place in the Championship race. Note the new low-profile canopy and the exhaust staining down the side on the *Omni Special.* (Emil Strasser)

C/n D.1171, N777L, returned to racing in September 1980 at Reno after its 1976 Mojave slide. *Rare Bear* qualified fourth and was given a 'did not start' because of gear, radio and engine problems. A mayday was declared and N777L landed on lap 5. The pilot was given the 'did not start' because he crossed the start line without a radio. (Emil Strasser)

C/n D.1171 at the 1988 Hamilton Air Races, California, where N777L and Lyle Shelton took first place in the Championship race at 412.492mph, with N777L wearing this brown paint scheme. (Jerry Liang)

C/n D.1171, N777L at the 1992 Reno Air Races during an engine test. *Rare Bear* wore a new emerald green and white paint scheme that proved to be unlucky as the 1992 race was won by arch rival Bill Destefani in #7 *Strega* and #77 DNF. (Bob Kennedy)

C/n D.1171, N777L, sporting a new gold paint scheme for the 1994–95 racing season. Lyle Shelton installed a further cut-down canopy and a cut-down, three-bladed prop for a Lockheed P-3 Orion. Seen at Van Nuys, California, in August 1994. (Russ Hiatt)

C/n D.1171, N777L, taxiing out at Nellis Air Force Base, Nevada, in November 2004. John Penny flew #77 in the Unlimited Demonstration race. Note that *Rare Bear* has reverted to a four-bladed prop. (Jerry Liang)

C/n D.1171, Race #77, and John Penny on their way out to win the 2007 Unlimited Gold race at Reno. The winning speed was 478.394mph. This was the last Gold win for N777L. (Jerry Liang)

C/n D.1171, N777L, at Reno 2009. It used a new boil-out cooling system that exhausted at the tail. It did not help #77 win as the Bearcat finished second in the Gold race at 479.088mph. *Rare Bear* raced another six years and had its best finish in the last year it raced when it placed second in the Gold for 2015. It is now in storage and owned by Rod Lewis. (Bob Kennedy)

# C/N D.1181

BuNo 121787 F8F-2P
Acceptance date: December 26, 1948
Delivery date: In delivery December 1948

To O&R BuAer M&S location illegible. To O&R BuAer M&S NAS San Diego, CA, on March 16, 1950. To O&R BuAer M&S NAS Alameda, CA, on May 29, 1950, with 20 hours TT[49]. To O&R BuAer M&S NAS Norfolk, VA, on September 24, 1950. To Composite Squadron Sixty-Two, VC-62, at NAS Norfolk with 29 hours TT. To NAS Jacksonville, FL, with VC-62 in November 1950. With VC-62 Det. 7 aboard the USS *Franklin D. Roosevelt*, CV-42, on November 5, 1950, as part of CVG-6. To NAS Cecil Field, FL, with VC-62 on May 16, 1951. With VC-62 Det. 5 aboard the USS *Midway*, CV-41, on December 8, 1951. Then with VC-62 Det. 32 aboard the USS *Tarawa*, CV-40, on December 23, 1951, with 606 hours TT. Back to NAS Cecil Field until June 10, 1952. Then assigned to VC-12 at NAS Quonset Point, RI. To O&R at NAS Norfolk on June 27, 1952. To NARTU Norfolk, October 28, 1952, with 723 hours TT. To NARTU Denver, CO, in August 1953 with 864 hours TT. To NARTU Norfolk, in February 1954 reporting 962 hours TT. To storage at NAF Litchfield Park, AZ, on October 18, 1955, with 979 hours TT. Stricken from inventory on August 27, 1956. Sold as surplus to John F. Carr[50] of Minneapolis, MN, for $505.00 at NAS North Island, CA, on April 14, 1959, and registered as N6821D. Carr was a vice president with Northwest Aerial Survey Inc based in Minneapolis. There are no indications that this Bearcat was ever modified for survey other than the reinstallation of the standard K-24 camera. Sold on September 22, 1958[51], to M. W. "Lee" Fairbrother[52]of Rosemount, MN, for "exhibition work," for $1.00 OVC. Sold April 29, 1966, to John W. Church[53] of Alameda, CA, who changed the registration to N148F on May 30, 1966. Bearcat N148F competed at Reno as Race #11 in 1966 with Chuck Klusman the pilot, and in 1967 with Church as pilot. By May 5, 1967, Church

C/n D.1181, BuNo 121787, F8F-2P, N6821D, perhaps at Minneapolis, Minnesota, in 1959 after being surplused from NAS North Island still wearing its Naval Air Reserve Training Unit (NARTU) Norfolk markings. Although sold to an aerial survey company, there is no evidence it was ever used for that work. (Dick Phillips Collection)

reported 1016.2 hours TT. Church sold N148F to Hawke Flying Service of Modesto of CA, on November 1, 1968. Walter "Bud" M. Fountain Jr. was the owner. Fountain stated on his application for "Experimental" registration that airframe had 1079.8 hours as of November 14, 1968. Fountain attempted to compete at Reno as Race #99, but was unsuccessful due to multiple engine issues. Bearcat N148F had 1090.8 hours TT. By January 1973 the aircraft had 1,094 hours TT, and in September Fountain returned to race at Reno as Race #24 after an extensive program to clean up the airframe and remove weight. He qualified tenth and was forced to drop out on lap 5 with a broken hydraulic line during the Gold race. A month later, on October 20, 1973, N148F fatally crashed during the Mojave Air Races after having an inflight fire. Registration canceled by the FAA on January 7, 1974.

---

49  This Bearcat may have been kept in a Pool until needed after delivery, or may have been involved in an accident that required repairs with M&S. Both would explain the low number of hours

50  This was John Carr's first of two F8Fs. He obtained c/n D.902 three months later in a trade/sale

51  Original Bill of Sale from the Navy to Carr shows April 14, 1959, while the Bill of Sale from Carr to Fairbrother is dated September 22, 1958. Documents date-stamped by the FAA show June 1, 1959, at 4:31pm, for both Bills of Sale. Obviously, there was a typographical error that was not caught

52  Fairbrother raced a P-38 and P-51 during the 1946 to 1949 National Air Races

53  Second of three John W. Church would own. The other Bearcats were c/n D.1122 and c/n D.1190

C/n. D.1181, N148F, Race #11, at Reno in September 1966, flown by Chuck Klusman. Race #11 had qualified seventh and finished fourth in the Consolation race at 342.74mph. (William T. Larkins)

C/n D.1181, N148F. For the 1967 Reno races John Church changed Race #11 paint scheme to this striking overall black with bronze Grumman Hawk down the side. Note how the paint has blistered and was peeling after N148F finished second in the Consolation race at 336.1mph. (Emil Strasser)

C/n D.1181, N148F, as Race #99, and with a new owner at the Reno races in September 1969. New owner Bud Fountain had stripped the Bearcat of its beautiful black and bronze paint with the exception of the tail, which was still black with white race numbers. Engine problems kept #99 out of competition that year. (William T. Larkins)

C/n D.1181, N148F, at Mojave, California, as Race #24 in October 1973 with Bud Fountain standing in the cockpit the day before his fatal crash. The overall polished natural metal finish and red trim with white cheat line looked fantastic. The name *Hawke Dusters* is carried on the cowling. (Jerry Liang)

# C/N D.1190

BuNo 122637 F8F-2
Acceptance date: December 30, 1948
Delivery date: In delivery December 1948

First notation of History Card, VF-91 with CVG-3 NAS Quonset Point, RI, in 1950. To VF-34 and CVG-3 NAS Quonset Point in 1950, exact date unknown, aircraft had 346 hours TT. To VF-74 and CVG-7 NAS Jacksonville, FL, on June 18, 1950, then back to VF-34 at NAS Quonset Point ten days later. By August, it was still with VF-34 and had 457 hours TT. To O&R BuAer M&S NAS Norfolk, VA, on December 21, 1951, with 528 hours TT. To NARTU Norfolk on February 6, 1952. To NART Birmingham, AL, on February 9, 1952. To FASRON 5 at NAS Oceana, VA, on May 27, 1952. To VF-742 at NAS Oceana on June 5, 1952. Aboard the USS *Midway*, CV-41, on July 20, 1952. To NART Birmingham on September 8, 1952. To Utility Squadron Two, VU-2, at NAS Quonset Point on May 4, 1953, with 665 hours TT. To VU-4 at Naval Air Test Station, NATS, Chincoteague, VA, in late May 1953 with 729 hours TT. To O&R

C/n D.1190, BuNo 122637, F8F-2, N1033B, on the ramp at Teterboro, New Jersey, January 22, 1967, while owned by New Jersey Air Service Co. The aircraft was stripped to bare metal and had its gun ports covered over. It was sold to Sherman Cooper in California a few months later. (Dick Phillips Collection)

BuAer M&S NAS Corpus Christi, TX, on October 24, 1953. To O&R BuAer M&S NAS San Diego, CA, on February 11, 1954. To O&R BuAer FA NAS San Diego on October 18, 1955. Retired on October 18, 1955. Stricken on January 9, 1957, with 752 hours TT. Sold as surplus May 27, 1958, one of several bought that day by Stinson Field Aircraft for $708.91 and registered as N1033B. Sold on August 27, 1958, to Transair Inc of Linden, NJ. Sold on November 30, 1961, to New Jersey Air Co of Hackensack, NJ, and reported as having last flown in July 1958. Sold on July 18, 1962, to Julius Moore of New York City for $7,000.00. Sold on August 11, 1962, to William Johnson of Miami, FL. Bearcat returned to New Jersey Air Co on September 27, 1965, via court order for mechanic's lien for unpaid work and because New Jersey Air was unable to deliver aircraft due to "non-airworthiness of aircraft and FAA will not issue a ferry permit." By April 1966,

aircraft reported to have 762 hours TT having only flown ten hours since being sold to Stinson at North Island, CA, and flown to Linden. Sold on September 28, 1967, to Dr. William S. Cooper[54] of Merced, CA. Sold on September 7, 1971, to John W. Church[55] of Monterey, CA, and reregistered as N198F. Church raced it at Reno in 1972 as Race #98. Sold on December 5, 1972, to John B. Gury[56] of St. Louis, MO. By February 1975, the Bearcat was reported as having 940 hours TT. Sold on March 20, 1978, to Cecil H. Harp, Jas L. Hayes and John A. Herlihy[57] of Canby, OR. Herlihy would race it at Reno in 1978 as Race #98. Sold on February 2, 1982, to Cinema Air of Carlsbad, CA. Thomas Freidkin used the Bearcat in some TV productions over the years. To Chino Warbirds/Comanche Warbirds Houston of TX, in July 2008. Registration changed to N8TF in 2009 and is currently flying.

---

54  Cooper may have intended to race it; it was on the ramp at Reno in 1969, but did not qualify or race. Cooper purchased and raced a modified Sea Fury instead

55  John W. Church purchased his third Bearcat

56  The first of two that John B. Gury owned and the one he kept the longest. He owned c/n D.1122 at the same time

57  Herlihy had also owned c/n D.1126

C/n D.1190, N1033B, at Reno, Nevada, during the 1969 races, one of five Bearcats there that year. The aircraft was shown by its new owner Sherman Cooper, but not raced. He would later race the modified #87 Hawker Sea Fury. (Jerry Liang)

C/n D.1190, as N198F sporting blue pseudo-military markings at Madera, California, in August 1978. Note how the roll-over structure has been removed and a second seat added. (Russ Hiatt)

C/n D.1190, N198F at the 1979 Reno Air Races as Race #98 and flown by John Herlihy, one of its owners. Number 98 qualified 12th at 371.35mph. Herlihy did not finish after two laps in the Championship race. (William T. Larkins)

C/n D.1190, N198F at Chino, California, in April 2004 after being repainted by its new owner Cinema Air. The markings are similar to those of the Naval Reserve Unit based at Jacksonville, Florida, in 1953. (Bob Kennedy)

C/n D.1190, had its registration changed to NX1TF in 2009 and is pictured at Chino, California, in April 2009. Currently owned by Comanche Fighters (Tom Friedkin). It flies regularly. (Jerry Liang)

# C/N D.1201

BuNo 122648 F8F-2
Acceptance date: January 27, 1949
Delivery date: In delivery January 1949

To Pool, location not legible. To O&R BuAer M&S NAS Alameda, CA, on March 9, 1950, with 175 hours TT. To storage at NAF Litchfield Park, AZ, on June 19, 1950. To O&R BuAer M&S NAS Alameda on August 10, 1950, with 181 hours TT. To NART Denver, CO, on November 9, 1950. To O&R BuAer M&S NAS Corpus Christi, TX, on November 2, 1952, with 460 hours TT. Back to NART Denver, on December 7, 1952. To O&R BuAer M&S NAS Corpus Christi on March 10, 1953. To O&R BuAer M&S NAS San Diego, CA, on June 5, 1953. To O&R BuAer FA NAS San Diego on August 31, 1956. To retirement on October 18, 1955. Stricken on January 9, 1957, with 526 hours TT. Sold as surplus on May 26, 1958, for $1,258.91[58] to Stinson Field Aircraft and registered as N1032B. Sold on July 24, 1959, to J. W "Bill" Fornof[59] of Houma, LA. In April 1960, Fornof had a K-25 aerial camera installed to comply with FAA requirements. He reported 531.6 hours TT on the airframe and 143.3 hours TT on the engine since major overhaul, having only flown 5.6 hours after leaving the Navy. The Bearcat was written off in a landing accident at Streator, IL, and destroyed by fire on October 9, 1960. Registration canceled by FAA November 1963. No photo found of this Bearcat.

---

58  Of the seven Bearcats Stinson Field Aircraft purchased in two days; this is the highest price it paid

59  This was the first of three that Fornof would own; he also had c/n D.982 and G-58B c/n D.1262

# C/N D.1227

BuNo 122674 F8F-2
Acceptance date: March 18, 1949
Delivery date: Not listed

First notation on History Card was to VF-63 with CVG-6 NAS Oceana, VA, with no date listed. To VF-92 with CVG-9 NAS Quonset Point, RI, on January 17, 1950. To VF-74 with CVG-7 at NAS Quonset Point in May 1950 with 330 hours TT. To O&R BuAer M&S NAS Norfolk, VA, on August 23, 1950, with 368 hours TT where it remained until June 10, 1951, flying only eight hours. To Naval Air Test Center (NATC), NAS Patuxent River, MD, and assigned to Research and Development (R&D) on June 21, 1951. To O&R BuAer M&S NAS Corpus Christi, TX, on December 19, 1952, with 604 hours TT. The Bearcat moved back to NATC Patuxent River with R&D. To O&R BuAer M&S NAS Corpus Christi in

C/n D.1227, BuNo 122674, F8F-2, N7825C just after leaving NAS North Island. This Bearcat last served with NARTU Norfolk, before being placed in storage in August 1955. It was sitting on the ramp at Acme Aircraft in 1958. (Brian Baker via Dave Menard)

February 1953. To NART NAS Lincoln, Nebraska (NB), on September 2, 1953. To O&R BuAer M&S NAS Corpus Christi in 1953. To NARTU Norfolk on February 2, 1954, with 702 hours TT. To O&R BuAer M&S NAS San Diego on April 7, 1954. To O&R BuAer FA NAS San Diego on August 31, 1955. Retirement was on October 19, 1955. Custodian O&R NAS San Diego. Stricken on January 9, 1957, with 751 hours TT. Sold as surplus on August 15, 1958, to Acme Aircraft Parts Inc of Compton, CA, and registered as N7825C. Sold in 1958 to E. D. Weiner of Los Angeles, CA. Sold in 1963 to Leo J. Demers of Aurora, OR. Sold in 1964 to Larry Hamilton of Sonoma, CA, same address as Hamilton Aircraft. To CCLU National Bank of Denver, CO, in 1965. To Richard S. Tobey of Newport Beach, CA, in 1966. To Keefe Corporation[60] of Pacific Palisades, CA, in 1968, and listed as an ineligible aircraft due to "no inspection reports for the last thirteen months." To Keat E. Griggers of Jamestown, CA, in 1968. To Paul Finefrock of Hobart, Oklahoma, in 1969. To Gary R. Levitz of Avalon, TX, in 1972. Sold/donated in 1973 to Confederate Air Force of Harlingen, TX. Damaged in an off airport landing on April 19, 1974, and again ten years later on April 19, 1984. This resulted in the shipment of the aircraft to Chino, CA, for repairs/overhaul. It made its first flight afterwards on December 17, 1991. Transferred to the Confederate Air Force Southern California Wing at Camarillo, CA, in 1992, and registered owner changed to American Air Power Heritage Flying Museum in Midland, TX. Currently it is undergoing a complete overhaul at Camarillo, CA.

---

60  This is the same Howard Keefe that raced P-51 *Miss America* Race #11

C/n D.1227, N7825C at Orange County Airport, California, in 1964, while owned by Hamilton Aircraft and for sale. (Emil Strasser)

C/n D.1227, N7825C in April 1971 at Addison, Texas, while owned by Paul Finefrock, who owned two P-51Ds before buying this Bearcat. He sold N7825C to Gary Levitz in 1972. (Pete Bulban via Jay Miller)

C/n D.1227, N7825C on the ramp at Harlingen, Texas, in October 1984. It was sold or donated to the Confederate Air Force in 1973. A-102 had two incidents causing damage while with that owner between 1973 and 1984. It was rebuilt at Chino after the last incident and flew again in 1991. (Bob Kennedy)

C/n D.1227, N7825C after overhaul, at Madera, California, in August 1994. It is assigned to the Commemorative Air Force Southern California Wing. (Bob Kennedy)

C/n D.1227, N7825C taking off from the USS *Carl Vinson*, CVN-70, during the commemoration celebration marking the 50th anniversary of the end of World War Two in October 1995. (Jim Dunn)

C/n D.1227 N7825C flying over Tracy, California, before going into a complete overhaul and rebuild with Commemorative Air Force Southern California Wing at Camarillo, California. (Jim Dunn)

# C/N D.1258

BuNo 122705 F8F-2
Acceptance date: May 27, 1949
Delivery date: Not listed

First notation on History Card, VF-151 with CVG-19 NAS Alameda, CA. To VF-192 with CVG-11 aboard the USS *Boxer*, CV-21, in May 1950. To FASRON-8 NAS Alameda on August 17, 1950, with 355 hours TT. To O&R BuAer M&S NAS Alameda on October 13, 1950. To NART Denver, CO, on July 26,1951. To NART NAS Birmingham, AL, on March 15, 1952. To FASRON 5 NAS Oceana, VA, in May 1952 with 543 hours TT. To VF-742 at NAS Oceana on June 5, 1952. To NARTU NAS Jacksonville, FL, on September 8, 1952, with 622 hours TT. To O&R BuAer M&S NAS Corpus Christi, TX, in February 1953 with 665 hours TT. To O&R BuAer M&S NAS San Diego on December 11, 1953. Retired on October 18, 1955. Custodian O&R San Diego. Stricken on January 9, 1957, with 678 hours TT. Donated to La Mesa-Spring Valley School District in La Mesa, CA, on November 25, 1957, for "Instructional use at the Fletcher Hills School Aircraft Program." It was registered as N4989V to La Mesa-Spring Valley School District. Aircraft was trucked to the Fletcher Hills school, a distance of about 35 miles, and not flown. Registration canceled at the request of owner on December 31, 1963, as the aircraft was sold to Ben Hammer (B&H Metal Co), 360 Bay Blvd in Chula Vista, CA, for scrap purposes on February 9, 1961. No photo found of this Bearcat.

# C/N D.1261

BuNo 122708 F8F-2
Acceptance date: May 31, 1949
Delivery date: June 22, 1950

This was the last F8F built. To B.A.R. Research Development and Engineering Department (RD&DE) at Bethpage, NY, on June 1, 1949. To NATC Patuxent River, MD, with RD&DE on June 22, 1950. To O&R BuAer M&S NAS Norfolk, VA, on December 6, 1950, with 198 hours TT. To NARTU NAS Norfolk on February 6, 1952, then to NART NAS Birmingham, AL, on February 9, 1952. To NARTU NAS Jacksonville, FL, in May 1952 with 247 hours TT. To O&R BuAer M&S NAS Corpus Christi, TX, on July 2, 1953, with 453 hours TT. To O&R BuAer M&S NAS San Diego, CA, on December 11, 1953. To O&R BuAer FA NAS San Diego on August 31, 1955. Retired on October 18, 1955. Stricken on January 8, 1957, with 460 hours TT. Sold as surplus on May 26, 1958, to E. D. Weiner of Los Angeles, CA, for $1,122.01 and registered as N7701C. Sold on November 23, 1958, to Ben Widtfeldt of Phoenix, AZ. Sold on December 30, 1958, to Rudolph Paslaski of Detroit, MI. Paslaski kept it for almost three years and flew it the most. Sold on September 24, 1965, to Michael J. Devanney of Cincinnati, OH, who had a K-21 camera installed for "aerial photo work[61]." Sold on April 26, 1968, to Chester F. Christopher[62] of New Shrewsbury, NJ. Sold on October 16, 1968, to Ronald E. Reynolds and Bert Howland of Norwalk, CT, who reported it as having 573.1 hours TT. It had only flown 113.1 hours since it was sold by the Navy. Sold on November 1, 1971, to John M. "Jack" Sliker of Wadley, GA. Sliker[63] modified N7701C for racing and competed from 1973 to 1975 at Miami, Reno and Mojave as Race #4. In its first race in 1973 at Miami, it was the top qualifier and later qualified fifth at Reno in 1973 and placed third in the 1975 Gold race. Jack Sliker was fatally injured in the crash of N7701C at Flagstaff, AZ, on September 16, 1975, on his way home from the Reno races. Registration canceled by FAA "as aircraft being totally destroyed." Remains were sold on April 4, 1985, to Elmer Ward[64] of Santa Ana, CA, who reinstated the registration number of June 20, 1986. Remains used in the rebuild of the Bearcat that became NL3025 (#2). Registration canceled at owner's request on March 24, 1996, as "aircraft scrapped."

C/n D.1261, BuNo 122708, F8F-2 as N7701C at Acme Aircraft Torrance, California, airport in July 1958. This was the last military Bearcat built. When stricken in January 1957 it had only 460hrs total time. No work was done as Acme was waiting for a Type Certificate. E. D. Weiner had paid $1,122.01 for the low-time aircraft. Note, there is another Bearcat behind it. (Dusty Carter)

---

61  This is perhaps the first time the Bearcat was given an Airworthiness Certificate and flown

62  This was Chester F. Christopher's third F8F. The others were c/n D.963 and c/n D.1105

63  Jack Sliker had raced P-51 Race #17 before in transcon and pylon races

64  Ward may have given some thought to using this number for his Bearcat project

C/n D.1261, N7701C at Wright-Patterson Air Force Base, Ohio, on May 19, 1967. Michael Devanney owned it before he sold it to Chester Christopher, who would apply an overall blue paint scheme with a broad white strip down the side. (Jay Miller Collection)

C/n D.1261, N7701C at the Reno Air Races for the first time in 1973. Owner Jack Sliker kept some of the blue paint from the previous owner on the right wing's outer panel, rudder, and horizontal stabilizer, while painting the left outer panel red. Note, the outer wing panels have not yet been clipped. (Emil Strasser)

C/n D.1261, N7701C at Reno in 1973 showing the blue side of *Escape II*. At the time, Race #4 had around 700hrs total time. Jack Sliker finished fourth in the Championship race, for which he collected $3,150.00. (Jay Miller Collection)

C/n D.1261, N7701C at the Reno Air Races in September 1974, its second year of racing. Its wings have now been clipped and painted all white. Like most racing Bearcats, it has an extended boat tail. Race #4 finished second in the Consolation race, earning Jack Sliker $1,786.00. (Jerry Liang)

C/n D.1261, N7701C at the October 1974 Mojave Air Races. The name *Escape II* carried over from Jack Sliker's Mustang racer Race #17 *Escape I*. This angle shows the top air intake and clipped wing tips to an advantage. (Emil Strasser)

C/n D.1261, N7701C in June 1975 at the Mojave race. The large carburetor intake has been removed, the rudder was white and the Southeastern Aircraft Inc titles under the canopy have been removed. Race #4 finished fourth in the Championship race. (Emil Strasser)

C/n D.1261, N7701C at Reno in September 1975 as Race #4 where it finished third in the Championship race. Jack Sliker was fatally injured in the crash of N7701C on his way home from the Reno races. (Jay Miller Collection)

# C/N D.1262

BuNo None G-58B
Delivery date: March 1949 to Grumman Aircraft Corp of Bethpage, NY, and registered N700A on October 25, 1949.

This was the second civil Bearcat, a Model G-58B, built by Grumman and flown as a company demonstrator by Grumman president Roger W. Kahn. This aircraft was part Dash-1, with a CA-15 engine and engine mounting and cowling, and Dash-2 fuselage and tall tail, with a baggage compartment and civil radios. With the retirement of Kahn, N700A was sold/donated on July 30, 1959, to Cornell University Aeronautics Laboratory in Buffalo, NY, for use as a "chase plane" and target. It was also used in the development of electronic gear, black boxes. At the time of sale, N700A was reported to have 381.07 hours TT. It was sold on March 19, 1969 to warbird collector William "Bill" Ross of Chicago, IL, for $22,200.00 with 448 hours TT. It sold again on March 28, 1969, to J. W. "Bill" Fornof of Houma, LA, as his third Cat. Fornof used N700A in a dual aerobatic routine with his son Corky. It was sold and registered on March 16, 1972, to John W. "Corky" Fornof Jr. following the death of his father in N7700C. By April 13, 1973, the aircraft was reported to have 818.2 hours TT. It sold on September 9, 1981, to Windward Aviation Inc, Champlin Fighter Museum, of Enid, OK, and was later moved to Mesa, AZ, and displayed. On January 3, 1986, it was sold to Robert J. Pond, Trustee of Spring Park, MN, and the Planes of Fame East Museum. It was registered in 1999 to Robert J. Pond of Palm Springs, CA and is currently on display at the Palm Springs Air Museum in a standard Navy blue paint scheme; it flies regularly.

C/n D.1262, G-58B, N700A was built at the end of F8F production and did not have any military equipment installed. It was flown by Grumman president Roger W. Kahn as a company demonstrator for sales promotions of Grumman aircraft and nicknamed *The Red Ship*. (Grumman Corp)

Upon Roger W. Kahn's retirement, Bearcat c/n D.1262, G-58B, N700A, was donated to Cornell University. *The Red Ship* is still wearing the Cornell Aeronautical Laboratory badge at the Milwaukee airport, Wisconsin, in July 1969, shortly after being sold to William "Bill" Ross. (Douglas Slowiak)

C/n D.1262, G-58B, N700A was built by Grumman as a company demonstrator and for the personal use of company president Roger W. Kahn. It was sold or donated to Cornell University's Aero Lab and flown until sold to Bill Ross, who then sold it to renowned airshow pilot J. W. "Bill" Fornof. This is a publicity photo of N700A and Fornof. (Harold F. Beal)

C/n D.1262 being towed at NAS Jacksonville, Florida, in 1973. N700A was flown by J. W. "Corky" Fornof Jr. after his father's 1971 death while flying Bearcat N7700C. Both Bearcats were painted alike. (L. B. Sides)

C/n D.1262, N700A at Oshkosh in 1987, now owned by Robert "Bob" Pond as part of his Planes of Fame East Air Museum. (Dick Phillips)

C/n D.1262, N700A repainted in a pseudo-military scheme at Palm Springs Air Museum, California, in 1999. It is kept in great condition and flies somewhat regularly. (Steve Ginter)

One other number must be added to this list, a mystery Bearcat and a possible 30th aircraft. In the FAA records there is a file for an F8F-2, complete with Bills of Sales, Applications for Registration, and correspondence with its owner starting in 1958 and ending in 1963. Presented is the information contained in the FAA file. The U.S. Navy History Card is missing; however, what is known is that this Bearcat served with VF-92 abroad the USS LEYTE (CV-32) where it suffered a crash-landing accident in June 1949 and later while assigned to VF-194 in 1950 it had another landing accident, nothing further is known. This Bearcat is:

# C/N D.1033

BuNo 122659, F8F-2
No delivery date, no stricken date or last squadron assignment.

The first item in this aircraft's FAA civil file is a Bill of Sale from Acme Aircraft Parts Inc. to Madden & Playford Aircraft Inc.[65], of 5353 N.W. 36 St. Miami, FL. for $1,650.00 on December 4, 1958. In the section of the Bill of Sale describing aircraft make and model it shows, Grumman-Model F8F-2 and the serial number is shown as, Bu No 122659. At some later date and using a different typewriter next to the make and model number, someone has typed N4993V and on the line for the serial number, s/n 121859 has been added. The Bill of Sale is signed by Louis Walter, President (of Acme Aircraft Parts), and the rest of the typing matches all other Acme Bills of Sale. It was received by the FAA on January 6, 1959.

The civil registration number falls into a block of assigned Grumman allocated registrations, while the new BuNo is for a Vought F4U-5 Corsair. This Corsair was assigned to VF-44 and went off a carrier deck into the sea near Norfolk, VA. in January 1951.

Next is an Application for Registration from Madden & Playford (a corporation) dated November 5, 1959, for Grumman F8F-2 N4993V, s/n 121859. Hand written across the top is "VOID SOLD." On the same day as the Application for Registration was signed by the VP of Madden & Playford, a Bill of Sale is signed for the sale of N-4993V for $1.00 OVC to Atlantic Aircraft Corporation of Palm Beach, FL. On November 5, 1959, Atlantic Aircraft Corp also filed an Application for Registration for N4993V, s/n 121859.

It should be noted that all of the Bills of Sale are stamped by the FAA as "Not Acceptable for Recording."

A Bill of Sale is executed on December 21, 1959, by Atlantic for the sale of N4993V for $1.00 OVC to John D. Clark of 3210 Love-Field Drive, Dallas, Texas.

The FAA sent Clark a letter dated January 18, 1960, with subject: Grumman N4993V and reads:

We received your bill of sale for registration of the subject aircraft. The aircraft cannot be registered in your name, and any documents submitted as evidence of your ownership cannot be recorded, pending compliance with the item(s) checked below:

(x) A check or money order for $4.00, made payable to the FAA.
(xx) A completely executed application signed in ink, must be submitted by you.
(xx) Documentary evidence of ownership of the aircraft from Acme Aircraft Parts, Inc., (previous owner).

There must have been ongoing conversations regarding this Bearcat as on November 12, 1963, the FAA finally tells Clark by certified letter:

Examination of the file for Grumman aircraft, serial number 121859, N4993V, indicates that this aircraft is unregistered. In order to register this aircraft in your name, we should be furnished the following:

A bill of sale to cover each change in ownership of the aircraft from the applicable military department to Acme Aircraft Parts Inc., or from Acme Aircraft Company, Lomita, California, to Acme Aircraft Parts, Inc., to complete the chain of ownership;

A duly executed application for registration in your name.

If, however, you do not desire registration in your name, please advise this office of your disposition of the aircraft.

The letter contains a hand-written note "Ret unclaimed 2 April 1960." In the file there is a copy of the Certified envelope sent to Clark that is marked "Returned to Sender" "No Such Address" dated November 26, 1960.

---

65  Madden & Playford were an aircraft broker and leasing company that bought and sold surplus aircraft mainly to Latin American countries. It was dissolved December 17, 1959.

The last entry in the file for N4993V BuNo 121859 (122659) is an Aircraft Accident Notice and under Section B, it reads that "The above Registration Number is to be canceled for reason checked below: Other: 'Admin Cancelled January 30, 1975.

So, why no Bill of Sale from the US Navy? What was sold by Acme in the first place? Why the change in BuNo and what happened to this aircraft?

It may be that an F8F-2 was bought by Acme for spare parts for use on their civil conversion projects and then sold as a complete non-flyable aircraft that passed through several owners and was never flown. Maybe the aircraft was complete and sold/exported from the US and not reported; Madden & Playford were known used-aircraft exporters. Clark could have done the same, or he could have broken it up for parts. There is also a rumor that an F8F was placed on display at NAS Dallas in the 1960s, at the base of the station's control tower and later scrapped. There are no known photos of this Bearcat.

# DRAWINGS AND DOCUMENTS

F8F-1, BuNo 94896, front view. (Grumman Corp)

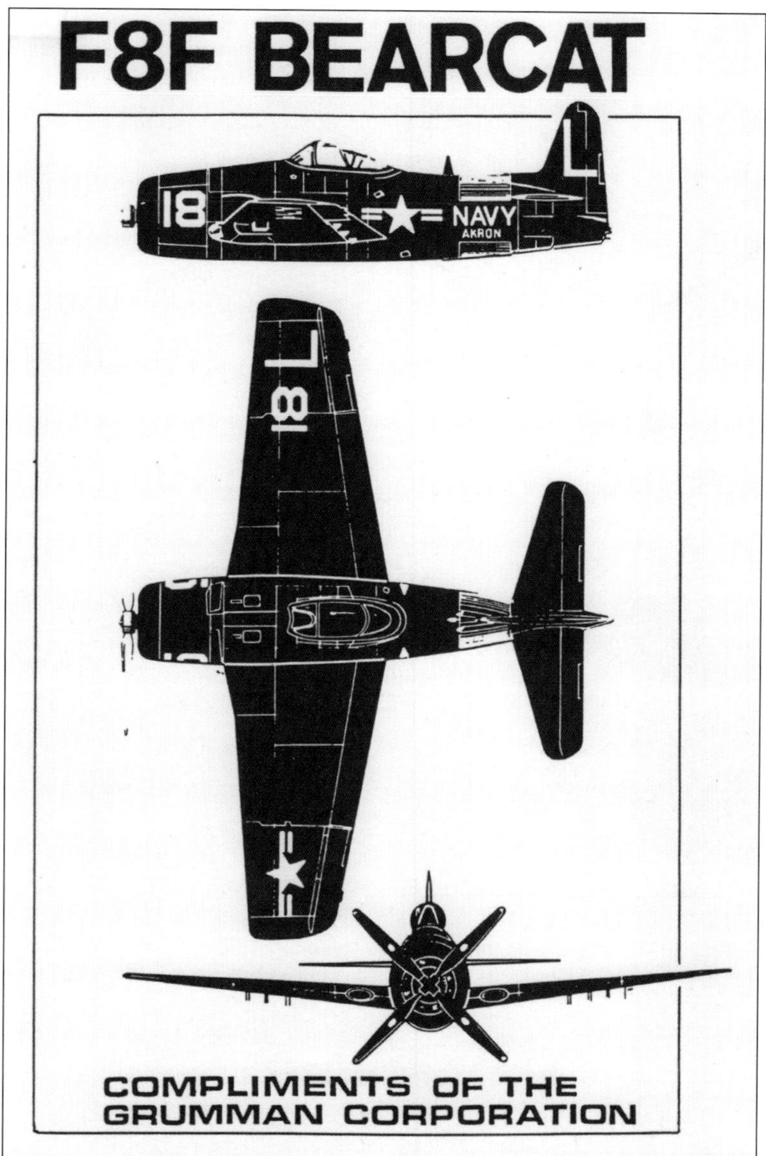



Handbook *AN 01-85FD-2* produced for the United States Navy by Grumman, detailing aircraft. (Provided by Grumman Aircraft Corporation)

# SECTION I
## DESCRIPTION, DIMENSIONS AND LEADING PARTICULARS

### 1. DESCRIPTION.

*a.* GENERAL. — The F8F airplane is a class VF single place, folding low wing fighter. It is designed for either land or carrier based operation including catapult take-off. Information on the following F8F models is included in this manual: F8F-1, F8F-1B, F8F-1N, F8F-2, F8F-2N and F8F-2P airplanes.

(1) The alighting gear, wing flaps, dive recovery flaps, gun chargers and oil cooler shutter doors are operated hydraulically. The cowl flaps are operated electrically. The arresting hook is extended manually. The wing outer panels are folded, spread, and locked manually by the ground crew.

(2) The F8F-1, -1B and -1N airplanes are powered by a Pratt & Whitney R-2800-34W single stage, two speed supercharged engine which is equipped with a water injection system. Later models are equipped with a manifold pressure regulator. Model F8F-2, -2P and -2N airplanes are powered by a Pratt & Whitney R-2800-30W variable speed supercharged engine equipped with water injection and an automatic engine control unit.

(3) The main self-sealing fuel cell, located beneath the cockpit floor, has a capacity of 185 gallons. A 150 gallon droppable fuel tank may be installed on the fuselage bomb rack and a 100 gallon droppable tank on each wing bomb rack.

(4) Armament for the F8F-1 and -1N airplanes consists of four .50 calibre guns located in the wing center section. The ammunition boxes are located outboard of the guns. The F8F-1B, -2 and -2N airplanes are equipped with four M-3 (T-31) 20mm guns. Two 20mm guns are installed in the F8F-2P airplanes. The wing structure of the airplanes has been altered accordingly to accommodate the 20mm installation. The ammunition compartments are part of the wing structure and folding doors in the wing upper surface provide access to the 20mm guns and the ammunition compartments. Provisions are made in all models for the installation of bombs underneath the wing center section. Pylons are provided for the installation of four rocket projectiles, two on each side of the wing center section. A "Tiny Tim" can be carried on each wing bomb rack.

(5) Airplanes up to ser No. 95103 inclusive are equipped with Radio System No. 9. Later F8F aircraft are furnished with Radio System No. 27. The night fighter models are identical to the day fighters except that AN/APS-19 radar equipment, a windshield degreasing installation, an MK 20 gunsight, Bu Ord No. 7229908 flash hider, exhaust flame damper, and either a GR-1 (F8F-1N) or a GR-2 (F8F-2N) automatic pilot are added.

### 2. PRINCIPAL DIMENSIONS.

*a.* GENERAL.
Span:

| | |
|---|---:|
| Wings spread | 35′ 6″ |
| Wings folded (max) | 23′ 9½″ |
| Height over tail, thrust line level | 13′ 2″ |
| Height over propeller—3-point position | 19′ 9″ |
| Height in hoisting attitude from top of sling to bottom of wheels | 11′ 10″ |
| Height (max), during wing folding operation | 13′ 1″ |
| Height (max), with wings folded | 12′ 11″ |
| Length (max), thrust line level | 27′ 6″ |
| Length from hoisting sling to furthest aft part of tail, thrust line level, rudder neutral, elevator down | 20′ 3″ |

*b.* WING.
Wing Chord:

| | |
|---|---:|
| At root section | 115.87″ |
| At construction tip section (6″ inboard actual tip) | 51.5″ |
| Wing incidence: | |
| At root section (to fuselage ref line) | —1½° |
| Sweepback leading edge of wing | 5° 5′ |

Description, dimension and leading particulars.

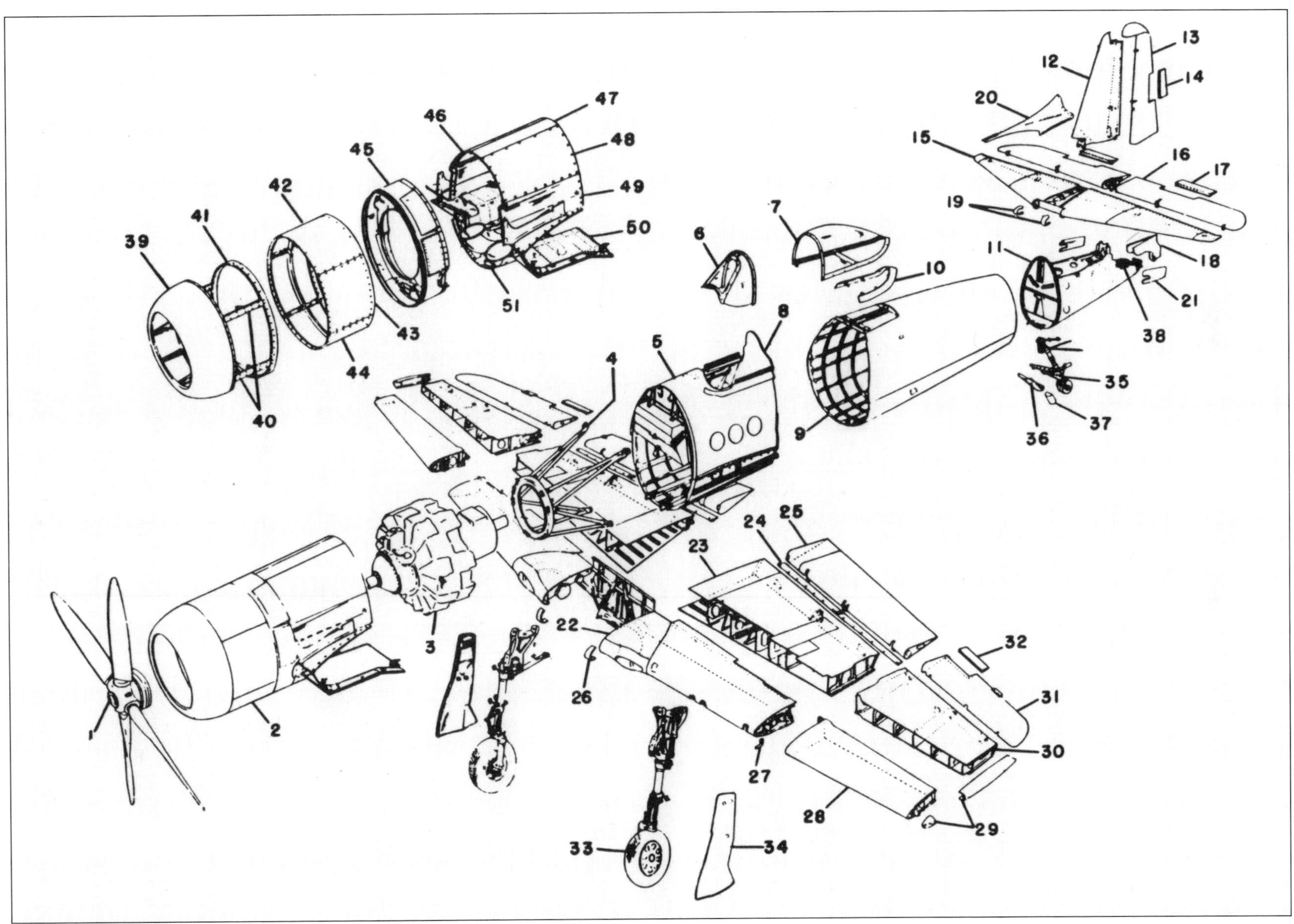

Exploded view of airplane.

| REF | ASSEMBLY NO. | TITLE OF ASSEMBLY | REF | ASSEMBLY NO. | TITLE OF ASSEMBLY |
|---|---|---|---|---|---|
| 1 | A642-G1 | Propeller (Aeroprop) F8F-1 | | 124830 | Pitot Tube (F8F-2) |
| | A642-G4 | Propeller (Aeroprop) F8F-2 | 28 | 53025 | Leading Edge Wing O. P. |
| 2 | 55000 | Cowling Installation | 29 | 53027 | Cap—Wing Tip |
| | 124100-1 | Cowling Installation | 30 | 53026 | Trailing Edge |
| 3 | 55300 | P & W Engine (R2800-34W) (F8F-1) | 31 | 53007 | Aileron (Structure) (F8F-1) |
| | | P & W Engine (R2800-30W) (F8F-2) | | 53007-18 | Aileron (Structure) (F8F-2) |
| 4 | 55110 | Mount—Engine | 32 | 53295 | Tab—Aileron (F8F-1) |
| | 124050 | Mount—Engine (BuAer 95379 up) | | 53295-1 | Tab—Aileron (F8F-2) |
| 5 | 54001 | Cockpit Section (Sta 101.012 to 146.25) | 33 | 54701 | Main Wheels Installation |
| 6 | 54015 | Windshield—Cockpit Section (F8F-1) | 34 | 54730 | Fairing—Main Wheel |
| | 124700 | Windshield—Cockpit Section (F8F-2) | 35 | 54702 | Tail Wheel Installation |
| 7 | 54008 | Hood—Cockpit Section—Cabin | 36 | 54709 | Fairing—Drag Strut |
| | 54480 | Hood—Cabin (BuAer 95104 up) | 37 | 24595 | Fairing—Tail Wheel Caster |
| 8 | 54402 | Armor—Cockpit Section (F8F-1) | 38 | 57200 | Gear (Instl)—Arresting |
| | 124086 | Armor—Cockpit Section (F8F-2) | 39 | 55002 | Spinning—Nose |
| 9 | 54002 | Mid-section (Sta 146.25 to 262.25) (F8F-1) | 40 | 55045-1 | Channel—Panel Support—Top (F8F-1) |
| | 54520 | Mid-section (Sta 146.25 to 262.25) (F8F-2) | | 55045-8 | Channel—Panel Support—Top (F8F-2) |
| | 124729 | Mid-section (Sta 146.25 to 262.25) (F8F-2P) | | 55045-10 | Channel—Panel Support—Top (F8F-2) |
| 10 | 54344 | Fairing—Mid-Section—Cabin Hood (Fixed) | | 55045-2 | Channel—Panel Support—Bottom (1L/1R) (F8F-2) |
| 11 | 54003 | Tail Section (Sta 262.25 to 328) | 41 | 55005 | Ring—Panel Support—Rear |
| | 54523 | Tail Section (BuAer 122087 up) | 42 | 55006 | Panel—Top |
| 12 | 53803 | Fin (F8F-1) | 43 | 55007 | Panel—Side (1L/1R) |
| | 53900 | Fin (F8F-2) | 44 | 55008 | Panel—Bottom (F8F-1) |
| 13 | 53804 | Rudder (Covered) (F8F-1) | | 124084-1 | Panel—Bottom (F8F-2) |
| | 53942 | Rudder (Covered) (F8F-2) | 45 | 55010 | Baffle (F8F-1) |
| 14 | 53807 | Tab—Rudder (F8F-1) | | 124100-1 | Baffle (F8F-2) |
| | 53970 | Tab—Rudder (F8F-2) | 46 | 55125 | Panel—Accessory Compartment—RH (F8F-1) |
| 15 | 53808 | Stabilizer | | 124090-2 | Panel—Accessory Compartment—RH (F8F-2) |
| 16 | 53810 | Elevator (Covered) | 47 | 55022 | Channel—Accessory Compartment—Top (F8F-1) |
| 17 | 53812 | Tab—Elevator | | 55022-4 | Channel—Accessory Compartment—Top (F8F-2) |
| 18 | 54016 | Fairing—Tail Cone | 48 | 55023 | Panel—Accessory Compartment—LH (F8F-1) |
| 19 | 53887 | Fairing—Stabilizer | | 124090-1 | Panel—Accessory Compartment—LH (F8F-2) |
| 20 | 53878 | Fairing—Dorsal Tail Fin to Fuselage | 49 | 55200 | Trough—Accessory Compartment Side Exhaust (1L/1R) (F8F-1) |
| | 53918 | Fairing—Dorsal Tail Fin to Fuselage (F8F-2) | | 124080-1 | Trough—Accessory Compartment Side Exhaust (1L/1R) (F8F-2) |
| 21 | 53889 | Doors—Fin Fairing—Access | 50 | 55019 | Door—Wheel Pocket (1L/1R) (F8F-1) |
| 22 | 53021 | Leading Edge Wing C. S. (F8F-1, -1N) | | 55019-3 | Door—Wheel Pocket (1L/1R) (F8F-2) |
| | 59021 | Leading Edge Wing C. S. (F8F-1B, F8F-2) | 51 | 55021 | Panel—Accessory Compartment Bottom (1L/1R) (F8F-1) |
| 23 | 59022 | Trailing Edge | | 124099-1 | Panel—Accessory Compartment Bottom (1L/1R) (F8F-2) |
| 24 | 53034 | Door—Flap Gap Closure | | | |
| | 53038 | Door—Flap Gap Closure—(BuAer 95029 up) | | | |
| 25 | 53019 | Flap (Covered) | | | |
| 26 | 55016 | Fairing—Leading Edge to Side Cowling (F8F-1) | | | |
| | 124123 | Fairing—Leading Edge to Side Cowing (F8F-2) | | | |
| 27 | 53301 | Pitot Tube (F8F-1) | | | |

Key to exploded view.

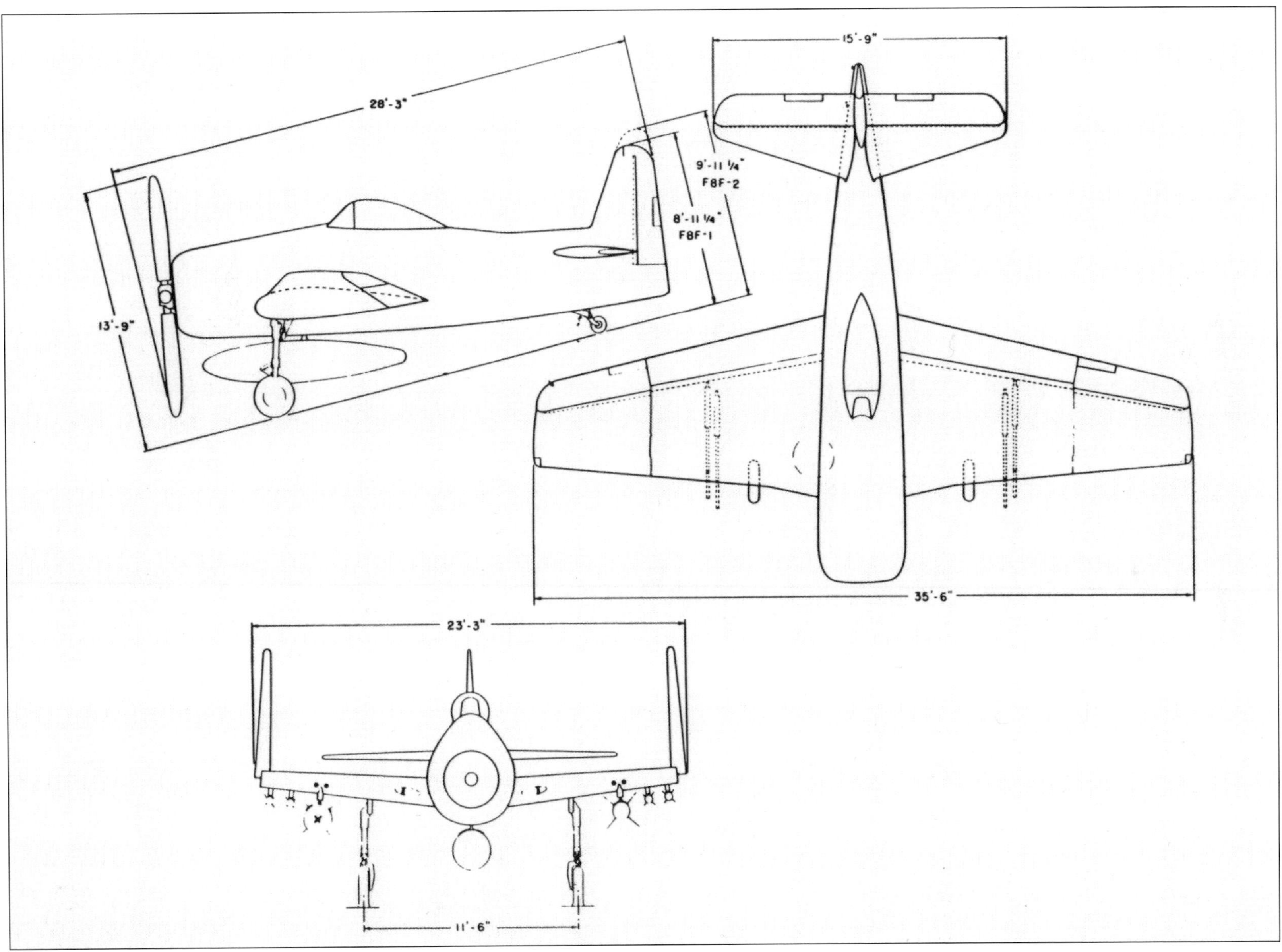


Dimensions diagram.

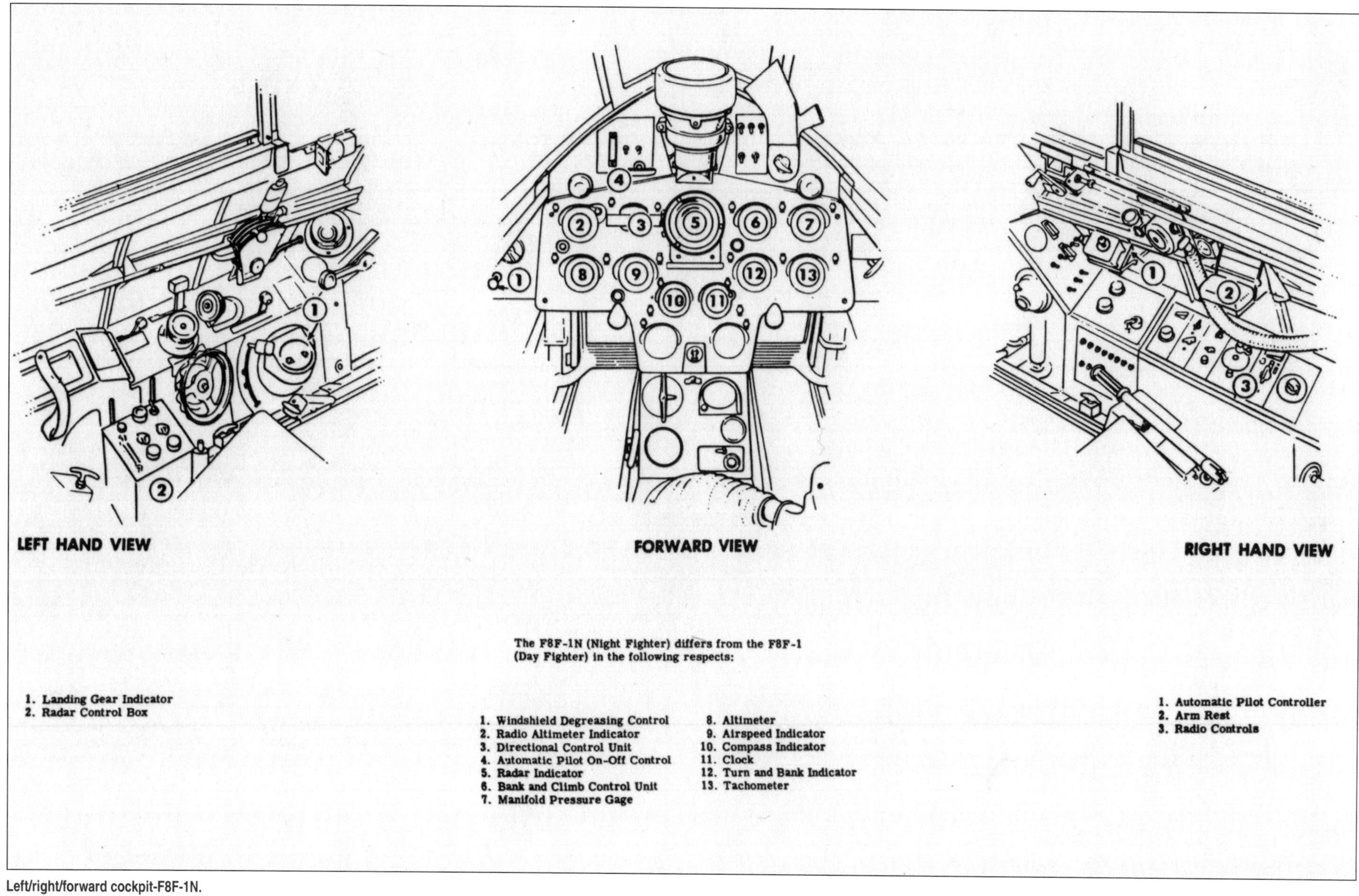



Left/right/forward cockpit-F8F-1N.

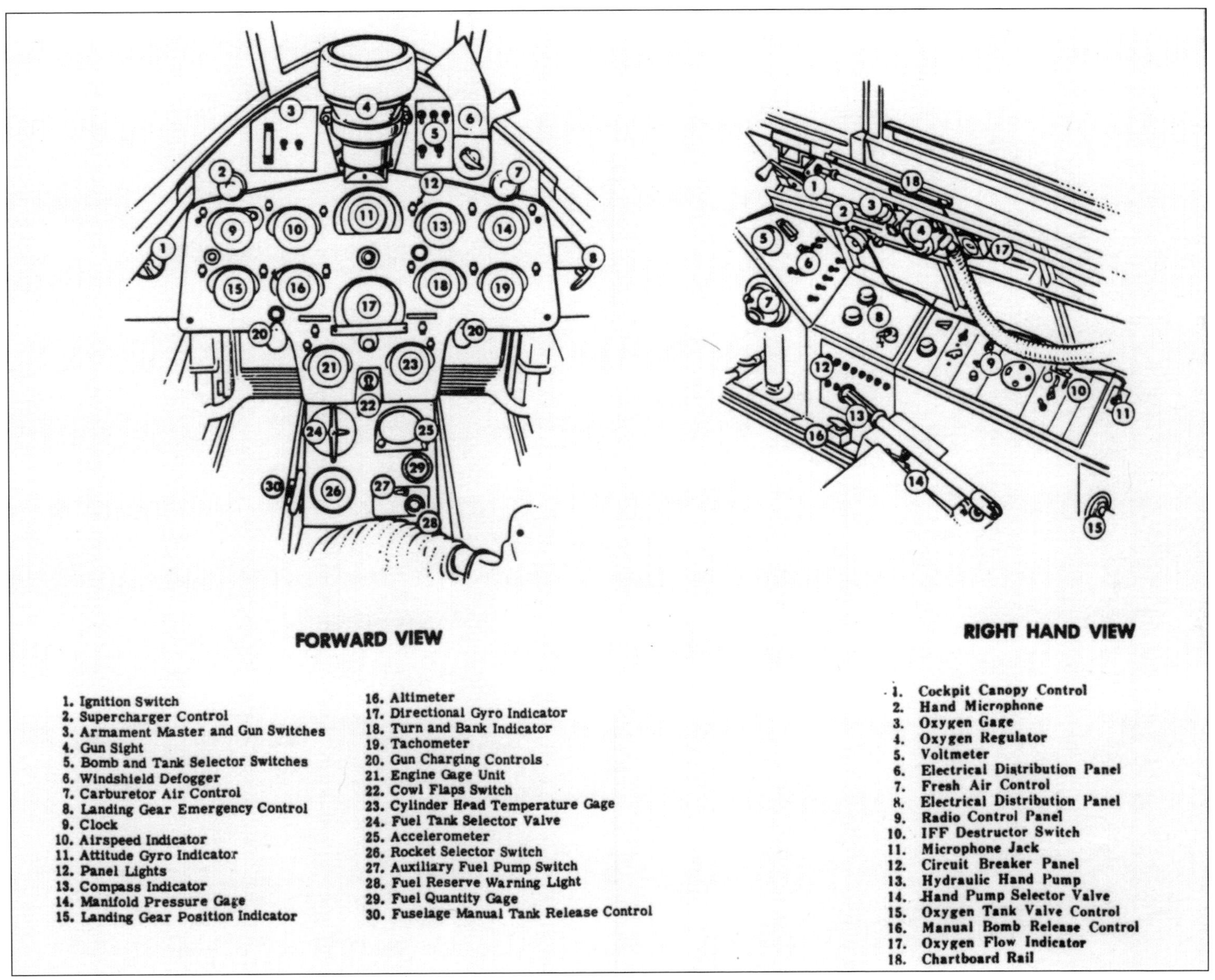



**FORWARD VIEW**

1. Ignition Switch
2. Supercharger Control
3. Armament Master and Gun Switches
4. Gun Sight
5. Bomb and Tank Selector Switches
6. Windshield Defogger
7. Carburetor Air Control
8. Landing Gear Emergency Control
9. Clock
10. Airspeed Indicator
11. Attitude Gyro Indicator
12. Panel Lights
13. Compass Indicator
14. Manifold Pressure Gage
15. Landing Gear Position Indicator
16. Altimeter
17. Directional Gyro Indicator
18. Turn and Bank Indicator
19. Tachometer
20. Gun Charging Controls
21. Engine Gage Unit
22. Cowl Flaps Switch
23. Cylinder Head Temperature Gage
24. Fuel Tank Selector Valve
25. Accelerometer
26. Rocket Selector Switch
27. Auxiliary Fuel Pump Switch
28. Fuel Reserve Warning Light
29. Fuel Quantity Gage
30. Fuselage Manual Tank Release Control

**RIGHT HAND VIEW**

1. Cockpit Canopy Control
2. Hand Microphone
3. Oxygen Gage
4. Oxygen Regulator
5. Voltmeter
6. Electrical Distribution Panel
7. Fresh Air Control
8. Electrical Distribution Panel
9. Radio Control Panel
10. IFF Destructor Switch
11. Microphone Jack
12. Circuit Breaker Panel
13. Hydraulic Hand Pump
14. Hand Pump Selector Valve
15. Oxygen Tank Valve Control
16. Manual Bomb Release Control
17. Oxygen Flow Indicator
18. Chartboard Rail

Left/right/forward cockpit-F8F-1/-1B.

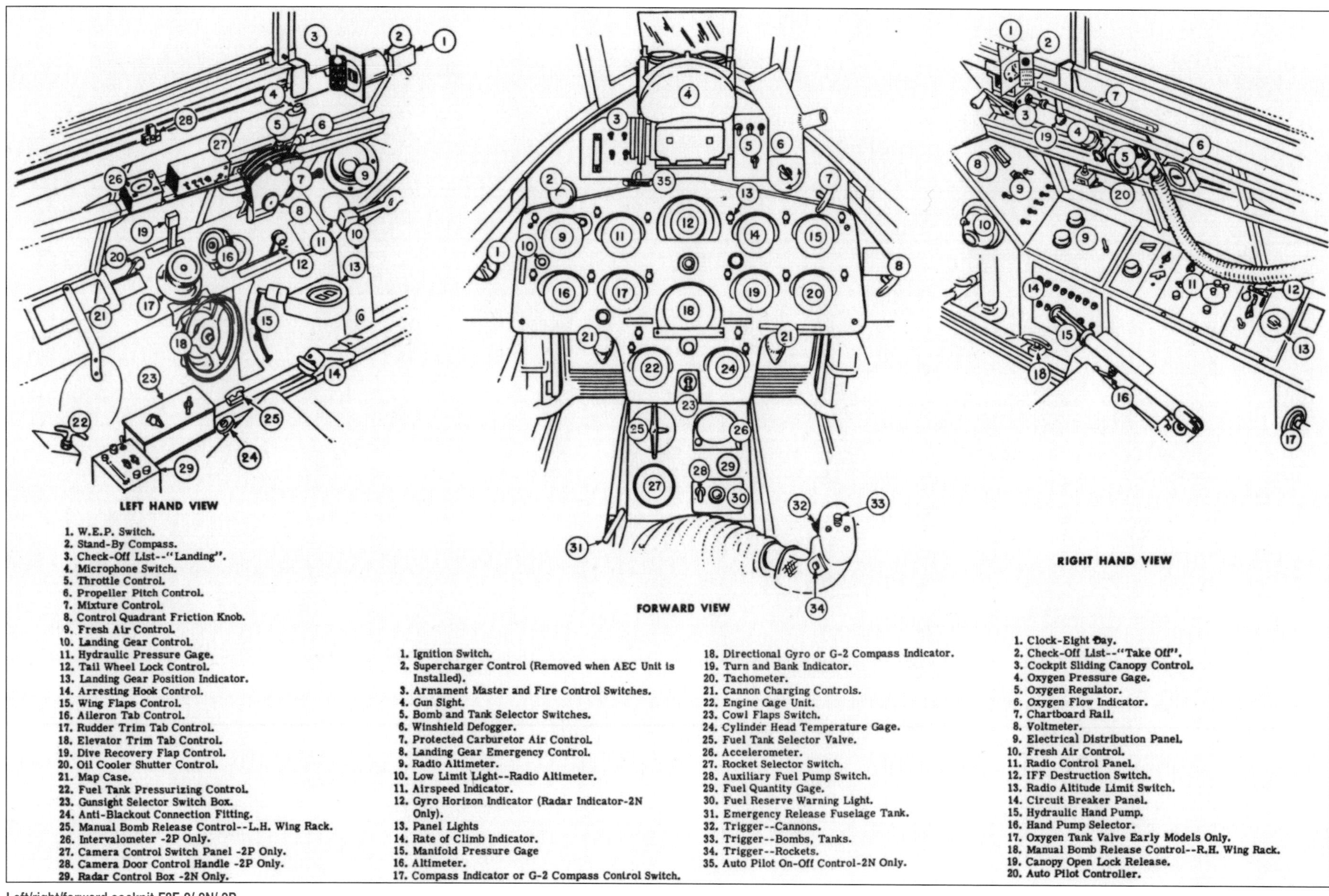


Left/right/forward cockpit-F8F-2/-2N/-2P.

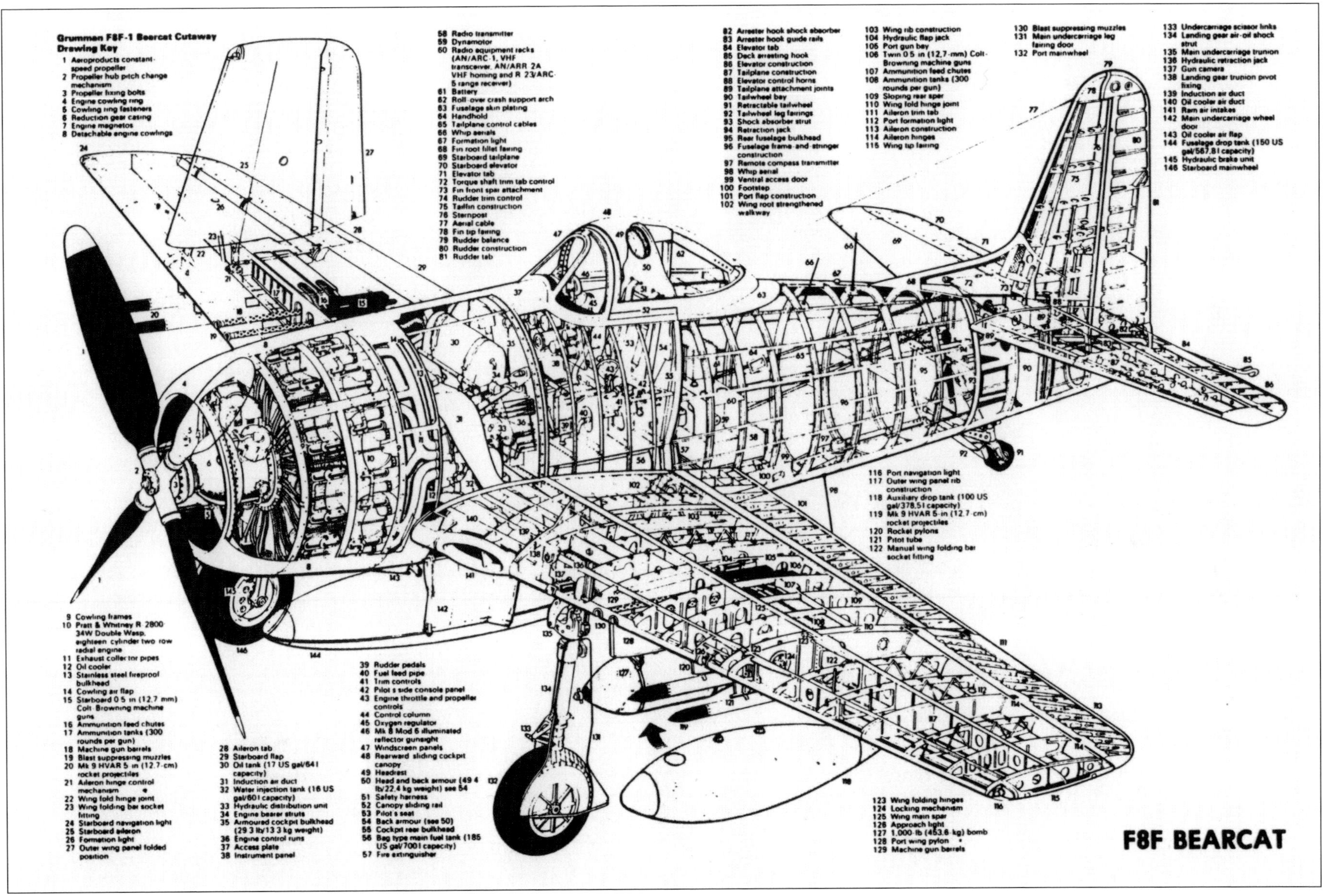


Cutaway F8F-1 (Note: Item 13 is the stainless-steel fireproof bulkhead. Item is the armored cockpit bulkhead weighing 293lb/133kg.)

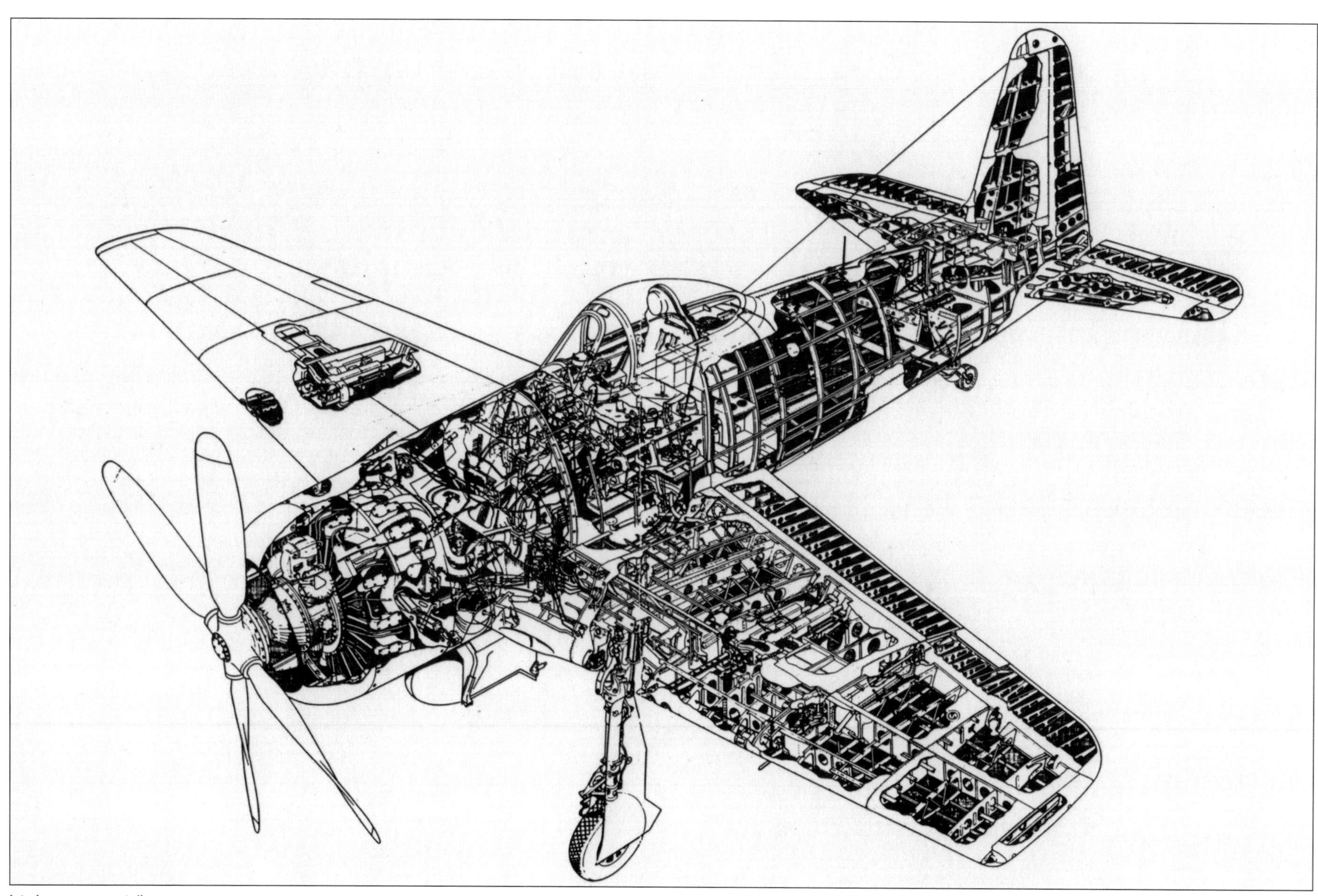

Interior arrangement diagram.

VICTOR        VICTOR          VICTOR          VICTOR

THIS CHANGE NOT EFFECTIVE UNTIL NOTIFICATION OF EFFECTIVE DATE BY BAUER

DEPARTMENT OF THE NAVY

BUREAU OF AERONAUTICS          Aer-AD-240
WASHINGTON 25, D.C.

Issue Date      27 May 1954
Effective Date_______________

F8F AIRCRAFT SERVICE CHANGE NO. 137

Subj:  Wing; reinforcement of the center section

Ref:   (a) Naval Aircraft Factory Model F8F Service Bulletin No. 3 of 11 Jun 53

1.  IDENTIFICATION:  This change is based on reference (a).  Copies of reference (a) may be obtained upon request from the NAMC (NAF) or the NAS (O&R), Corpus Christi.

2.  REASON FOR CHANGE:  To increase the strength of the centersection of the wing and extend the useful life of the wings for repeated application of high loads.

3.  APPLICATION:  This change is applicable to all F8F-1/2 series aircraft.

    a.  The activity having custody of aircraft at time of incorporation of change shall confirm incorporation of this change by a log book entry, describing and identifying the change by Model F8F Aircraft Service Change No. 137.

4.  WHEN CHANGE IS TO BE MADE:  This change is CLASS VICTOR and shall be accomplished in all applicable aircraft only at next overhaul.  Aircraft withdrawn from Bureau of Aeronautics Long Term Storage Pools are to have this change incorporated by the overhaul or modification activities prior to issue to the service.

5.  DESCRIPTION AND INSTALLATION INSTRUCTIONS:  This change consists of:  (a) installing two reinforcement bars (NAF 501631-1 & -2) nesting in the lower capstrip of the main beam wing center section between the port and starboard landing gear ribs, (b) Installing a strap hinge assembly (NAF 605126-2) on the lower surface of the wing for approximately 134 inches on both sides of the center line,  (c) installation of a guard plate (NAF 501635-9) over the center section wing reinforcement to prevent chafing of the fuel tank, (d) the installation of miscellaneous reinforcements and fastenings in connection with (a) and (b).

    a.  MAN-HOURS REQUIRED PER AIRCRAFT:  This change requires approximately 320 man-hours of work, if the airplane is stripped sufficiently for a major overhaul.

    b.  INSTALLATION INSTRUCTIONS:  This change shall be accomplished in accordance with the instructions contained in reference (a).

    c.  PARTS REQUIRED PER AIRCRAFT:  As listed in reference (a).

    d.  PARTS REQUIRED PER SPARE:  None.

    e.  PARTS TO BE REMOVED PER AIRCRAFT:  As listed in reference (a).

    f.  SPECIAL TOOLS, JIGS OR TEMPLATES REQUIRED:  As listed in reference (a).

VICTOR        VICTOR          VICTOR          VICTOR

---

Aer-AD-240

F8F AIRCRAFT SERVICE CHANGE NO. 137

6.  WEIGHT AND BALANCE DATA:  The effect of this change on the Basic Weight and Moment is as follows:

| POUNDS WEIGHT | INCHES AFT OF REFERENCE DATUM | MOMENT/1000 |
|---|---|---|
| *NET CHANGE 63 INCREASE | 101 | 6.4 INCREASE |

*Enter on Chart C of AN 01-1B-40 Handbook of Weight and Balance Data.

7.  SOURCE OF PARTS:  The parts and material necessary for this change shall be obtained from local stock or through normal supply channels.

    a.  SPECIAL TOOLS, JIGS OR TEMPLATES REQUIRED:  Shall be requisitioned through normal supply channels.

8.  DISPOSITION OF DISPLACED MATERIAL:  The displaced material shall be disposed of in accordance with existing disposal directives.

(signed)

R. W. Waymouth
By direction

*Left*: Department of the Navy, Bureau of Aeronautics (Aer-AD-240) from May 27, 1954. "F8F Aircraft Service Change NO.137" Subj: Wing: reinforcement of the center section." (Note: This is the two-page air directive regarding installation of the spar cap.)

*Above*: Page two of AER-AD-240.

This notice appeared in the June, 1949 issue of *Naval Aviation News*.

"A unique feature of the F8F Bearcat, the jettisonable wing tips, is being abandoned.

When the fighter was first introduced, it came out with about three feet of each wing tip designed so that it would pull off if the pilot exceeded operating G restrictions by a significant amount during violent maneuvers. The wing tips came off all right, but sometimes only one would break off. This led to a momentary uncontrollable roll and subsequently made it a little difficult to fly the airplane.

Later, a dual-jettison feature, consisting of a detonating cap and a length of prima-cord was put in each wing tip. (F8F Change #27). It was installed so that if one tip failed the cap and prima-cord would be fired on the other tip, thereby weakening it so it also would fail. A number of pilots have made landings safely in Bearcats with tips off, although a bit 'hot' because of reduced wing area.

Difficulties were met with maintenance of the jettisonable wing tip, coupled with the mental hazard of having an explosive charge in the wing. After slightly more than four years of service experience it was decided the disadvantages outweighed the good points of jettisoning. Change #90 was issued directing operating activities to remove the charge and increase the riveting on wing tips of all F8F's."

** From the Summer 1963 issue of *American Aviation Historical Society Journal*.

*Above left*: This notice appeared in the June 1949 issue of *Naval Aviation News*.

*Above right*: Early aircraft history card (NavAer-1925) for c/n D.10, BuNo 90446, XF8F-1, that became N14HP. Entries are hand written.

*Right*: Aircraft history card for c/n D. 628, BuNo 95356, F8F-1, that became N4752Y. "ABD VALLEY FORGE" means it made a cruise aboard the USS *Valley Forge* in October 1948.

**Card No. 1** — Contract Number: 8449 · Acceptance: Day 18 Mo 11 Yr 48 · Model: F8F 2 · Serial Number: 121776 · **STRICKEN**

| Card | Reporting Custodian — Name | Location | Cont. Cust. Code | | Status | Action Code | Control | Y: Date of Inventory (Day Mo Yr) | Number of Tour | Y: Age in Months | Y: Accumulated Hrs. in Tour | Y: Accumulated Hrs. Since Acceptance | Y |
|---|---|---|---|---|---|---|---|---|---|---|---|---|---|
| N | VF 113   CVG 11 | SAN DIEGO | 21 | 2 | A1 | | | | 1 | 039 | | | |
| N | FASRON 11 | SAN DIEGO | 21 | 2 | B | R | | 28030 | 1 | 049 | | | |
| P | FASRON 11 | SAN DIEGO | 21 | 2 | B | | | 50 | 1 | 12 | 306 | 324 | 3 |
| N | FASRON 8 | ALAMEDA | 21 | 2 | B | R | | 06060 | 1 | 049 | | | |
| P | FASRON 8 | ALAMEDA | 21 | 2 | B | | | 80 | 1 | 12 | 311 | 329 | |
| S | O&R BUAER M&S | ALAMEDA | 88 | 2 | E | R | | 13100 | 1 | 100 | | | |
| N | O&R BUAER M&S | ALAMEDA | 88 | 2 | EP | C | | 06110 | 1 | 100 | | | |
| P | O&R BUAER M&S | ALAMEDA | 88 | 2 | EP | | | 110 | 1 | 12 | 312 | 330 | |
| N | O&R BUAER M&S | ALAMEDA | 88 | 2 | E | C | | 18041 | 1 | 100 | | | |
| P | O&R BUAER M&S | ALAMEDA | 88 | 2 | EP | C | | 21 | 1 | 12 | 312 | 330 | |
| | O&R BUAER M&S | ALAMEDA | 88 | 2 | D1 | C | | 14051 | 1 | 100 | | | |
| P | O&R BUAER M&S | ALAMEDA | 88 | 2 | D1 | | | 51 | 1 | 12 | 0312 | 330 | |
| N | O&R BUAER M&S | ALAMEDA | 88 | 2 | B | C | | 02081 | 1 | 100 | | | |
| N | O&R BUAER M&S | ALAMEDA | 88 | 2 | C | C | | 09081 | 1 | 100 | | | |
| N | O&R BUAER M&S | NORFOLK | 88 | 2 | C | R | | 13081 | 1 | 100 | | | |
| N | VMT 1 | CHERRY POINT | 19 | 2 | A4 | R | | 24081 | 2 | 081 | | | |
| N | FASRON 8 | ALAMEDA | 21 | 2 | B | R | | 28081 | 2 | 081 | | | |
| N | VMT 1 | CHERRY POINT | 19 | 2 | A4 | E | | 29081 | 2 | 081 | | | |
| | VMFT 20 | CHERRY POINT | 19 | 2 | A4 | R | | 23012 | 2 | 033 | | | |
| | VMT 1 | CHERRY POINT | 19 | 2 | A4 | | | 111 | 2 | 03 | 25 | 375 | 1 |
| | VMFT 20 | CHERRY POINT | 19 | 2 | A4 | | | 22 | 2 | 06 | 47 | 337 | |
| | VMFT 20 | CHERRY POINT | 19 | 2 | A4 | | | 52 | 2 | 09 | 182 | 432 | 2 |
| | VMFT 20 | CHERRY POINT | 19 | 2 | A4 | | | 62 | 2 | 12 | 312 | 562 | 4 |
| | NAS NART | BIRMINGHAM | 50 | 2 | A4 | R | | 12092 | 2 | 013 | | | |
| | O&R BUAER M&S | CRPS CHRISTI | 88 | 2 | E | R | | 03013 | 2 | 013 | | | |
| | NAS NART | BIRMINGHAM | 50 | 2 | A4 | | | 112 | 2 | 00 | 335 | 585 | |
| | O&R BUAER M&S | CRPS CHRISTI | 88 | 2 | D1 | C | | 03023 | 2 | 013 | | | |
| | O&R BUAER M&S | CRPS CHRISTI | 88 | 2 | D1 | | | 023 | 2 | 16 | 344 | 594 | |

Aircraft history card (OP-NAV 50-157) for c/n D.1162, BuNo 121776, F8F-2, that became N68RW. Note the assignment to VMT-1 and VMFT-20, the two USMC Training Squadrons at MCAS Cherry Point, NC.

**Card No.** 1 | **Contract Number** 9241 | **Day/Mo/Yr** BO 12 48 | **Model** F8F 2 | **Serial Number** 122637 | **STRICKEN** | *N198F* (handwritten)

| Reporting Custodian | Station | Cust. Code | 2 | Status | Action Code | Date of Inventory / Action | No. Tour | Age in Months | Accum. Hrs in Tour | Accum. Hrs Since Acceptance | Flown 1 | Flown 2 | Flown 3 | Serial |
|---|---|---|---|---|---|---|---|---|---|---|---|---|---|---|
| VF 34 | CVG 3 QUONSET PNT | 11 | 2 | A | | 50 | 1 | 16 | 346 | 346 | 63 | 2 | 33 | 122637 |
| VF 74 | CVG 7 JACKSONVILLE | 11 | 2 | A1 | R | 18060 | 1 | 039 | | | | | | 122637 |
| VF 34 | CVG 3 QUONSET PNT | 11 | 2 | A1 | R | 28060 | 1 | 039 | | | | | | 122637 |
| VF 34 | CVG 3 QUONSET PNT | 11 | 2 | A | | 80 | 1 | 19 | 457 | 457 | 72 | 22 | 16 | 122637 |
| OIR BUAER M&S | NORFOLK | 88 | 2 | EP | R | 01120 | 1 | 120 | | | | | | 122637 |
| VF 34 | CVG 3 QUONSET PNT | 11 | 2 | A | | 110 | 1 | 22 | 525 | 525 | 23 | 22 | 23 | 122637 |
| OIR BUAER M&S | NORFOLK | 88 | 2 | D | C | 29120 | 1 | 120 | | | | | | 122637 |
| OIR BUAER M&S | NORFOLK | 88 | 2 | B0 | C | 27051 | 1 | 120 | | | | | | 122637 |
| OIR BUAER M&S | NORFOLK | 88 | 2 | D1 | | 21 | 1 | 22 | 524 | 526 | 2 | | | 122637 |
| VIR HUAER M&S | NORFOLK | 98 | 2 | B0 | | 51 | 1 | 22 | 0524 | 528 | 2 | | | 122637 |
| OIR BUAER M&S | NORFOLK | 88 | 2 | NY | C | 07061 | 1 | 120 | | | | | | 122637 |
| OIR BUAER M&S | NORFOLK | 88 | 2 | MZ | C | 27081 | 1 | 120 | | | | | | 122637 |
| OIR BUAER M&S | NORFOLK | 88 | 2 | H7 | C | 23101 | 1 | 120 | | | | | | 122637 |
| OIR BUAER M&S | NORFOLK | 88 | 2 | G7 | C | 15111 | 1 | 120 | | | | | | 122637 |
| OIR BUAER M&S | NORFOLK | 88 | 2 | B | C | 21121 | 1 | 120 | | | | | | 122637 |
| MARTU | NORFOLK | 50 | 2 | A4 | R | 06022 | 2 | 073 | | | | | | 122637 |
| NAS MART | BIRMINGHAM | 50 | 2 | A4 | R | 09022 | 2 | 073 | | | | | | 122637 |
| OIR BUAER M&S | NORFOLK | 88 | 2 | G7 | | 111 | 1 | 22 | 524 | 528 | | | | 122637 |
| NAS MART | BIRMINGHAM | 50 | 2 | A4 | | 22 | 2 | 01 | 5 | 536 | 1 | | 8 | 122637 |
| NAS MART | BIRMINGHAM | 50 | 2 | A4 | | 52 | 2 | | 30 | 561 | 11 | 15 | | 122637 |
| FASRON 5 | OCEANA | 11 | 2 | G5 | R | 27052 | 2 | 073 | | | | | | 122637 |
| VF 742 | OCEANA | 11 | 2 | A1 | R | 05062 | 2 | 073 | | | | | | 122637 |
| VF 742 | ABD MIDWAY | 11 | 2 | AJ | C | 20072 | 2 | 073 | | | | | | 122637 |
| VF 742 | ABD MIDWAY | 11 | 2 | A1 | C | 27072 | 2 | 073 | | | | | | 122637 |
| VF 742 | OCEANA | 11 | 2 | A1 | | 82 | 2 | 7 | 105 | 657 | 29 | 23 | 20 | 122637 |
| NAS MART | BIRMINGHAM | 50 | 2 | A4 | R | 08092 | 2 | 073 | | | | | | 122637 |

AIRCRAFT HISTORY CARD

Aircraft history card, page 1, for c/n D.1190, BuNo 122637, F8F-2, that became N198F. Note VF-742 aboard the USS *Midway* June to July 1952.

Page 2 for c/n D.1190, BuNo 122637 shows an assignment to VU-2 at NAS Chincoteague, VA, and Total Time of 752hrs at the time it was stricken from the inventory at NAS San Diego, CA.

122705    N4989V

| CONTRACT NUMBER | ACCEPTANCE (DAY MO. YR.) | MODEL | SERIAL NUMBER |
|---|---|---|---|
| 9241 | 27 0B 49 | F8F 2 | 122705 |

**STRICKEN**

| REPORTING CUSTODIAN — NAME | LOCATION | CONT. CUST. CODE | | STATUS | ACTION CODE | CONTROL | Y: DATE OF INVENTORY (DAY MO. YR.) | NUMBER OF TOUR | Y: AGE IN MONTHS | Y: ACCUMULATED HRS. IN TOUR | Y: ACCUM. HRS. SINCE ACCEPTANCE | HOURS FLOWN THREE MONTHS 1 | 2 |
|---|---|---|---|---|---|---|---|---|---|---|---|---|---|
| 151 CVG 19 | ALAMEDA | 21 | 2 | A1 | | | | 1 | 069 | | | | |
| 192 CVG 11 | ABD BOXER | 21 | 2 | A | | | 50 | 1 | 11 | 229 | 247 | 20 | 43 |
| RON 8 | ALAMEDA | 21 | 2 | B | R | | 17080 | 1 | 069 | | | | |
| RON 8 | ALAMEDA | 21 | 2 | B | | | 80 | 1 | 14 | 337 | 355 | 44 | 4 |
| BUAER M&S | ALAMEDA | 88 | 2 | E | R | | 13100 | 1 | 100 | | | | |
| BUAER M&S | ALAMEDA | 88 | 2 | EP | C | | 08110 | 1 | 100 | | | | |
| BUAER M&S | ALAMEDA | 88 | 2 | EP | | | 110 | 1 | 14 | 338 | 355 | 1 | |
| BUAER M&S | ALAMEDA | 88 | 2 | E | C | | 22031 | 1 | 100 | | | | |
| BUAER M&S | ALAMEDA | 88 | 2 | D1 | C | | 18041 | 1 | 100 | | | | |
| BUAER M&S | ALAMEDA | 88 | 2 | EP | | | 21 | 1 | 14 | 338 | 355 | | |
| BUAER M&S | ALAMEDA | 88 | 2 | D1 | | | 51 | 1 | 14 | 0358 | 355 | | |
| BUAER M&S | ALAMEDA | 88 | 2 | NY | C | | 26061 | 1 | 100 | | | | |
| BUAER M&S | ALAMEDA | 88 | 2 | B | C | | 16071 | 1 | 100 | | | | |
| | DENVER | 50 | 2 | A4 | R | | 26071 | 2 | 081 | | | | |
| NART | BIRMINGHAM | 50 | 2 | A4 | | | 15032 | 2 | 013 | | | | |
| NART | DENVER | 50 | 2 | A4 | | | 111 | 2 | 04 | 139 | 496 | 71 | 5 |
| NART | DENVER | 50 | 2 | A4 | | | 22 | 2 | 07 | 156 | 212 | 11 | 6 |
| RON 5 | OCEANA | 11 | 2 | B | | | 52 | 2 | 10 | 197 | 543 | 6 | 11 |
| RON 5 | OCEANA | 11 | 2 | GS | R | | 27052 | 2 | 013 | | | | |
| VF 742 | OCEANA | 11 | 2 | A1 | R | | 05062 | 2 | 013 | | | | |
| VF 742 | OCEANA | 11 | 2 | A1 | | | 02 | 2 | 13 | 262 | 619 | 24 | 34 |
| TU | JACKSONVILLE | 50 | 2 | A4 | R | | 08092 | 2 | 013 | | | | |
| BUAER M&S | CRPS CHRISTI | 88 | 2 | E | R | | 13013 | 2 | 013 | | | | |
| TU | JACKSONVILLE | 50 | 2 | A4 | | | 112 | 2 | 00 | 265 | 622 | | |
| BUAER M&S | CRPS CHRISTI | 88 | 2 | E | | | 023 | 2 | 17 | 308 | 665 | 17 | 6 |
| BUAER M&S | CRPS CHRISTI | 88 | 2 | E | | | 053 | 2 | 17 | 308 | 655 | | |
| BUAER M&S | CRPS CHRISTI | 88 | 2 | D1 | C | | 17093 | 2 | 013 | | | | |
| BUAER M&S | CRPS CHRISTI | 88 | 2 | E | | | 83 | 2 | 017 | 308 | 665 | | |

Aircraft history card, page 1, for c/n D.1258, BuNo 122705, that became N4989V. Its first assignment was to CVG-19 at NAS Alameda, CA, in 1950 and then aboard the USS *Boxer* in May 1950.

*122708    N7701C*

| Card No. | Contract Number | Day | Mo. | Yr. | Model | Serial Number | | |
|---|---|---|---|---|---|---|---|---|
| 1 | 9241 | 31 | 05 | 49 | F8F 2 | 122708 | STRICKEN | |

| Reporting Custodian (Name) | Location | Cont. Cust. Code | | Status | Action Code | Control | Date (Day/No./Yr.) | No. of Tour | Age in Mo. | Accum. Hrs. in Tour | Accum. Hrs. Since Acceptance | Y |
|---|---|---|---|---|---|---|---|---|---|---|---|---|
| ~~BAR RD&DE~~ | ~~BETHPAGE~~ | 70 | 2 | A9 | | | | | | | | |
| NATC RD&DE | PTXNT RIVER | 70 | 2 | A | | | 50 | 1 | 11 | 29 | 29 | 3 |
| NATC RD&DE | PTXNT RIVER | 70 | 2 | A9 | R | | 2060 | 1 | 079 | | | |
| NATC RD&DE | PTXNT RIVER | 70 | 2 | A | | | 80 | 1 | 14 | 102 | 102 | |
| O&R BUAER M&S | NORFOLK | 88 | 2 | EP | R | | 06120 | 1 | 120 | | | |
| O&R BUAER M&S | NORFOLK | 88 | 2 | D | C | | 16120 | 1 | 120 | | | |
| NATC RD&DE | PTXNT RIVER | 70 | 2 | A | | | 110 | 1 | 17 | 198 | 198 | 26 |
| O&R BUAER M&S | NORFOLK | 88 | 2 | BQ | C | | 19031 | 1 | 120 | | | |
| O&R BUAER M&S | NORFOLK | 88 | 2 | 01 | | | 21 | 1 | 18 | 204 | 204 | 5 |
| O&R BUAER M&S | NORFOLK | 88 | 2 | BG | | | 51 | 1 | 18 | 0204 | 207 | 3 |
| O&R BUAER M&S | NORFOLK | 88 | 2 | NY | C | | 07061 | 1 | 120 | | | |
| O&R BUAER M&S | NORFOLK | 88 | 2 | MZ | C | | 17071 | 1 | 120 | | | |
| O&R BUAER M&S | NORFOLK | 88 | 2 | H7 | C | | 18101 | 1 | 120 | | | |
| O&R BUAER M&S | NORFOLK | 88 | 2 | G7 | C | | 06111 | 1 | 120 | | | |
| O&R BUAER M&S | NORFOLK | 88 | 2 | B | C | | 06121 | 1 | 120 | | | |
| NARTU | NORFOLK | 50 | 2 | A4 | R | | 05022 | 2 | 073 | | | |
| NAS NART | BIRMINGHAM | 50 | 2 | 04 | R | | 09022 | 2 | 073 | | | |
| O&R BUAER M&S | NORFOLK | 88 | 2 | G7 | | | 111 | 1 | 18 | 204 | 208 | |
| NAS NART | BIRMINGHAM | 50 | 2 | A4 | | | 22 | 2 | 01 | 4 | 213 | |
| NARTU | JACKSONVILLE | 50 | 2 | A4 | | | 52 | 2 | | 38 | 247 | |
| NARTU | JACKSONVILLE | 50 | 2 | A4 | R | | 30042 | 2 | 073 | | | |
| NARTU | JACKSONVILLE | 50 | 2 | A4 | | | | | | 150 | 359 | 27 |
| NARTU | JACKSONVILLE | 50 | 2 | A4 | | | 112 | 2 | 00 | 193 | 402 | 28 |
| NARTU | JACKSONVILLE | 50 | 2 | A4 | | | 023 | 2 | | 211 | 420 | |
| NARTU | JACKSONVILLE | 50 | 2 | A4 | | | 053 | 2 | 00 | 235 | 444 | 17 |
| O&R BUAER M&S | CRPS CHRISTI | 88 | 2 | E | R | | 02073 | 2 | 073 | | | |
| O&R BUAER M&S | CRPS CHRISTI | 88 | 2 | E | | | 83 | 2 | 017 | 243 | 453 | 10 |

Page 1 of the aircraft history card for c/n D.1261, BuNo 122708, the last F8F Bearcat built. It became N7701C and was assigned to NATC Patuxent River, MD, with RD&DE and later to several NART/NARTUs.

| CARD NO. | CONTRACT NUMBER | ACCEPTANCE DAY MO. YR. | MODEL | SERIAL NUMBER | DATE STRICKEN |
|---|---|---|---|---|---|
| 2 | 9241 | 31 05 49 | F8F 2 | 122708 | |

| REPORTING CUSTODIAN NAME | LOCATION | CONT. CUST. CODE | | STATUS | ACTION CODE | CONTROL | Y: DATE OF INVENTORY DAY MO. YR. | NUMBER OF TOUR | MO. YR. / Y: AGE IN MONTHS | Y: ACCUMULATED HRS. IN TOUR | Y: ACCUMULATED HRS. SINCE ACCEPTANCE |
|---|---|---|---|---|---|---|---|---|---|---|---|
| O&R BUAER M&S | CRPS CHRISTI | 88 | 2 | D1 | C | | 02103 | 2 | 073 | | |
| O&R BUAER M&S | CRPS CHRISTI | 88 | 2 | D1 | | | 113 | 2 | 017 | 243 | 453 |
| O&R BUAER M&S | CRPS CHRISTI | 88 | 2 | B | C | | 08123 | 2 | 073 | | |
| O&R BUAER M&S | CRPS CHRISTI | 88 | 2 | C | C | | 09123 | 2 | 073 | | |
| O&R BUAER M&S | SAN DIEGO | 88 | 2 | NY | R | | 11123 | 2 | 073 | | |
| O&R BUAER M&S | SAN DIEGO | 88 | 2 | NY | | | 24 | 2 | 17 | 243 | 460 |
| O&R BUAER M&S | SAN DIEGO | 88 | 2 | MZ | C | | 24054 | 2 | 073 | | |
| O&R BUAER FA | SAN DIEGO | 88 | 2 | MZ | | | 310852 | 2 17 | 17 | 243 | 400 450 |
| O&R BUAER FA | SAN DIEGO | 88 | 2 | S3 | X | | 18105 | 2 | 73 | | |
| O&R BUAER FA | SAN DIEGO | 88 | 2 | S3 | | | 290262 | | 17 | 243 | 460 |

Page 2 for c/n D.1261, BuNo 122708, N7701C, showing it at NAS San Diego, CA, on October 18, 1955, having flown only 460hrs since acceptance and awaiting disposal.

FORM ACA-500 (PART C) (7-58)   (DUPLICATE)

U. S. DEPARTMENT OF COMMERCE—CIVIL AERONAUTICS ADMINISTRATION

## BILL OF SALE

For and in consideration of $505.00 the undersigned owner of the full legal and beneficial title of the aircraft described as follows:

AIRCRAFT MAKE AND MODEL

Grumman F8F-2

SERIAL NO.   Bureau #121787     REGISTRATION MARKS   N—682I D

does this 14th day of April 1959 hereby sell, grant, transfer, and deliver all of his right, title and interest in and to such aircraft unto:

(Name and address of purchaser—same as on Parts A and B of this form)

John F. Carr
4612 - 34th Ave. So.
Minneapolis, Minn.

and to his executors, administrators, and assigns, to have and to hold singularly the said aircraft forever, and certifies that same is not subject to any mortgage or other encumbrance except

| TYPE OF ENCUMBRANCE | AMOUNT | DATE |
|---|---|---|
| None | | |
| IN FAVOR OF | | |

In testimony whereof ______ have set ______ hand and seal this ______ day of ______ 19 ______ U. S. Naval Air Station,

NAME OF SELLER North Island, San Diego 35, Calif.

BY (SIGN IN INK) J. C. ANNALORO
(If executed for co-ownership, all must sign)

TITLE Contracting Officer
(If signed for a corporation, partnership, owner, or agent)

### ACKNOWLEDGMENT

State of California
County of San Diego

On this 20th day of April 1959 before me personally appeared the above named seller, to me known to be the person described in and who executed the foregoing bill of sale, and acknowledged that he executed the same as his free act and deed, and, if said bill of sale be that of a corporation swore that he was duly authorized to execute the same. Given under my hand and official seal the day and year written above.

(SEAL)

MY COMMISSION EXPIRES Aug. 12, 1960         Charles E. Drasil   NOTARY PUBLIC

FORWARD THIS COPY TO WASHINGTON — Retain Duplicate Copy.

Bill of Sale for c/n D.1181, BuNo 121787, N6821D, to John F. Carr of Minneapolis, MN. Purchase price was $505.00. This was the first of two he would obtain.

---

For and in consideration of $708.91 the undersigned owner of the full legal and beneficial title of the aircraft described as follows:

DOC. RECORDED

AIRCRAFT MAKE AND MODEL

Grumman - F8F-2

SERIAL NO.   Bureau #121731     REGISTRATION MARK   N1028B

does this 26th day of May 1958 hereby sell, grant, transfer, and deliver all of his right, title and interest in and to such aircraft unto:

(Name and address of purchaser—same as on Parts A and B of this form)

Stinson Field Aircraft
Box 1738
San Antonio 6, Texas

and to his executors, administrators, and assigns, to have and to hold singularly the said aircraft forever, and certifies that same is not subject to any mortgage or other encumbrance except

| TYPE OF ENCUMBRANCE | AMOUNT | DATE |
|---|---|---|
| none | | |
| IN FAVOR OF | | |

In testimony whereof ______ have set ______ hand and seal this ______ day of ______ 19 ______ U.S. Naval Air Station,

NAME OF SELLER North Island, San Diego 35, California

BY (SIGN IN INK) J. C. ANNALORO
(If executed for co-ownership, all must sign)

TITLE Contracting Officer
(If signed for a corporation, partnership, owner, or agent)

### ACKNOWLEDGMENT

State of California
County of San Diego

On this 10th day of June 1958 before me personally appeared the above named seller, to me known to be the person described in and who executed the foregoing bill of sale, and acknowledged that he executed the same as his free act and deed, and, if said bill of sale be that of a corporation swore that he was duly authorized to execute the same. Given under my hand and official seal the day and year written above.

NOTARY PUBLIC   Charles E. Drasil        MY COMMISSION EXPIRES   August 12, 1960

(SEAL)

FORWARD THIS COPY TO WASHINGTON — Retain Duplicate Copy.

Bill of Sale for c/n D.1105, BuNo 121731, to Stinson Field Aircraft of San Antonio, TX. It is one of two the company purchased that day, followed by four more the next day. Notice how registration number N1028B is written in instead of being typed in, meaning it was added later. Sold three months later to Transair in New Jersey for $10.00 OVC.

FEDERAL AVIATION AGENCY

FORM APPROVED
BUDGET BUREAU NO. 04-R082.

## APPLICATION AND AUTHORIZATION FOR FERRY PERMIT

### 1. APPLICATION

INSTRUCTIONS: Submit in duplicate to authorized Federal Aviation Agency representative or designated manufacturing inspection representative.

**DESCRIPTION OF AIRCRAFT**

| REGISTERED IN NAME OF | ADDRESS |
|---|---|
| N.R. HANSON & CHESTER CHRISTOPHER | 27 REEDS ROAD, NEW SHREWSBURY, NEW JERSEY |

| MAKE | MODEL |
|---|---|
| GRUMMAN | F8F |

| MANUFACTURER'S SERIAL NO. | IDENTIFICATION MARK |
|---|---|
| 121731 | N-500B |

**DESCRIPTION OF FLIGHT**

| FROM | TO |
|---|---|
| ASBURY PARK, N. J. | TETERBORO, N. J. |

| VIA | DATE | DURATION |
|---|---|---|
| DIRECT | 1/2/65 | 10 DAYS |

PURPOSE

AIRCRAFT TO BE WEIGHED.

I hereby request authority to ferry the above-described aircraft for the flight specified.

TELEPHONE REQUEST

*Chester Christopher* (SIGNATURE OF APPLICANT) — OWNER (TITLE) — 12/29/64 (DATE)

### 2. AUTHORIZATION

INSTRUCTIONS: Retain this authorization in aircraft for duration of flight. This is your authority to conduct the flight requested above. This permit is valid until landing is effected at the destination indicated in your request, provided the aircraft is flown by a properly certified crew, is operated in accordance with applicable Civil Air Regulations, and in accordance with the following special limitations:

1. THIS FLIGHT SHALL BE MADE IN ACCORDANCE WITH VISUAL FLIGHT RULES (DAY) ONLY, AND SHALL BE LIMITED TO PERSONNEL ESSENTIAL TO THE FLIGHT AND THEIR BAGGAGE.

2. THIS AUTHORIZATION IS VALID UPON CERTIFICATION IN THE AIRCRAFT LOG BOOK BY AN A&P MECHANIC, AFTER INSPECTION, THAT THE AIRCRAFT IS AIRWORTHY FOR THIS FLIGHT.

3. THIS PERMIT VALID FOR ONE (1) FLIGHT ONLY AND SHALL EXPIRE UPON ARRIVAL AT DESTINATION, BUT NOT LATER THAN SUNSET ON: JANUARY 12, 1965.

4. THE PILOT MUST BE PROPERLY RATED AND QUALIFIED.

5. THIS FERRY AUTHORIZATION SHALL BE CARRIED IN THE AIRCRAFT AT ALL TIMES DURING FLIGHT.

REMARKS:

| DATE ISSUED | SIGNATURE OF FAA REPRESENTATIVE | DESIGNEE NO. |
|---|---|---|
| 12/29/64 | WALTER H. SMITH | |

An example of an application for a ferry permit, in this case for c/n D.1105, now N500B. Notice its flight limitations and that it is only authorized for ten days. This is typical of ferry permits.

---

# Acme Aircraft Company

TORRANCE MUNICIPAL AIRPORT
P.O. BOX 516, LOMITA, CALIFORNIA
PHONE LOMITA 2050

September 17, 1959

Federal Aviation Agency
P. O. Box 90007 – Airport Station
Los Angeles 45, California

Dear Sirs:

Please issue an experimental license for a Grumman F8F2, aircraft No. N7700C, serial No. 121608 for the purpose of conducting our flight tests prior to submitting it to the F.A.A.'s Pilot for his evaluation for certification under Part 8 of the Civil Air Regulations.

We desire to use flight test area No. 2, which is closest to our facility. These flight tests will be conducted in accordance with the Visual Flight Rules.

Very truly yours,

C. R. Keeney

CRK:jku

The Torrance Airport is requested for all operations.

Copy of the original letter sent to the FAA by Roger Keeney, Acme Aircraft, requesting a license for c/n D.982, BuNo 121608, on September 17, 1959, as N7700C. This was the first F8F-2 to be civil registered. The request is for flight testing prior to applying for certification.

## FEDERAL AVIATION AGENCY

### OPERATING LIMITATIONS

#### Grumman Model F8F2, SERIAL NO. 121608, REG. NO. N-7700C

This placard must be displayed in the cockpit in full view of the pilot.

This aircraft must be operated in compliance with the following operating limitations:

1. All flights must be conducted in compliance with the requirements of Civil Air Regulation 60.12 and 60.24.

2. The only flights authorized are for the purpose of showing compliance with the Civil Air Regulations.

3. Persons or property shall not be carried for compensation or hire.

4. Occupancy of the aircraft is restricted to persons essential to the purpose of the flight.

5. Flights shall be limited to Torrance Municipal Airport, Torrance, California, and flight test area number 2. Flights between test area and airport shall be planned to involve the least exposure to persons and property on the ground.

6. All take-offs and landings to be on runway 25. All flights to be VFR.

7. Flight tests (Civil Air Regulation 60.60) shall not be conducted during flights outside of test area.

8. This authorization shall expire on March 17, 1960.

September 17, 1959

*Leland E. Safford*

Leland E. Safford
Supervising Inspector
AEDO-48

---

## FEDERAL AVIATION AGENCY

AR-32
Page 1
GRUMMAN
F8F-2

November 23, 1959

### TYPE CERTIFICATE DATA SHEET NO. AR-32

This data sheet which is a part of type certificate No. AR-32 prescribes conditions and limitations under which the product for which the type certificate was issued meets the airworthiness requirements of the Civil Air Regulations.

— Type Certificate Holder    ⟩ Acme Aircraft Company ⟨
           Lomita, California

#### I Model F8F-2 (Restricted Category), Approved November 2, 1959

Engine       P&W R-2800-30W

Fuel       115/145 or 100/130 Minimum grade aviation gasoline

Engine limits       Low - inter. - high impeller ratio. A.E.C.
      7.29    9.15      10:55

|  | HP | RPM | MP In.Hg. | Alt. |
|---|---|---|---|---|
| Maximum continuous | 1700 | 2600 | 44.0 | S.L. |
| 115/145 Fuel | 1800 | 2600 | 44.0 | 6000 |
|  | 1450 | 2600 | 44.0 | 22000 |
| *Military Power | 2250 | 2800 | 60.0 | S.L. |
| *Military Power | 2090 | 2800 | 57.0 | 6000 |
| *Military Power | 1550 | 2800 | 56.0 | 22000 |
| Maximum continuous | – | 2600 | 44.0 | S.L. |
| 100/130 Fuel | – | 2600 | 44.0 | 6000 |
|  | – | 2600 | 44.0 | 22600 |
| *Military Power | – | 2800 | 55.0 | S.L. |
| *Military Power | – | 2800 | 55.0 | 6000 |
| *Military Power | – | 2800 | 55.0 | 22000 |

*Takeoff Power

| Propeller | Aeroproducts Model No. A642-G4 |
|---|---|
|  | Blade No. H20C1-162-11M5 or H20F-162-11M5 |

Airspeed limits       Never exceed (Under 10,000 feet)   487 m.p.h. (425 knots) I.A.S.
      With Landing Gear extended        160 m.p.h. (140 knots) I.A.S.
      With Flaps extended           254 m.p.h. (220 knots) I.A.S.
      Reduce $V_{NE}$ 2 knots/1000 feet above 10,000 feet

| C.G. range | (+20.0) (19.26% M.A.C.) to (+25.9) (26.% M.A.C.) |
|---|---|
| Empty wt. C.G. range | None |
| Datum | Wing leading edge (35 in. outboard of fuselage sta. 68.57) |
| M.A.C. | 87.55 in. (L.E. M.A.C. +3.1 in. aft of datum) |
| Leveling means | Lugs inside fuselage at sta. 196 and 213 |
| Maximum weight | 10,200 lb. |
| No. of seats | 1 (+83.5) |
| Maximum baggage | None |

---

Letter from FAA providing "operating limitations" for flight testing of c/n D.982, N7700C, addressed to Acme Aircraft for flights. Limitation no 5 says, "planned to involve the least exposure to persons and property on the ground."

First page of "Type Certificate Data Sheet No AR-32" issued November 23, 1959, giving the "Type Certificate for Grumman F8F-2" to Acme Aircraft Co of Lomita, CA, and Roger Keeney.

AR-32 Page 1 (Back)

| | |
|---|---|
| Fuel capacity | 185 gal. - Main Fuselage<br>150 gal. - Droppable Type Fuselage<br>100 gal. - Droppable Type Wing<br>(See NOTE 4 for restrictions on auxiliary fuel tanks) |
| Oil capacity | 17 gal. |
| Other operating limitations | Buaer Pilot's Handbook An-01-85FD-1 |
| Control surface<br>movements | Wing flaps               Down 40°<br>Aileron tab   Up    5° Down 5°<br>Aileron       Up  23° Down 21°<br>Elevator tab  Up   8° Down 20°<br>Elevator     Up  23° Down 13½°<br>Rudder tab   Right 17° Left 17°<br>Rudder      Right 31° Left 24° |
| Serial Nos. eligible | 121523 through 122708 |
| Certification basis | CAR 8 as amended to October 11, 1950.<br>Type Certificate No. AR-32 issued November 2, 1959<br>  for the special purpose of aerial photography.<br>Date of application for Type Certificate October 20, 1958. |
| Production basis | None. No aircraft may be produced under this approval. |
| Equipment | The basic required equipment as prescribed in the applicable airworthiness regulations (see certification basis) must be installed in the aircraft for certification. In addition, equipment necessary for the special purpose of aerial photography must be installed. |

NOTE 1. Current weight and balance report including list of equipment included in certificated empty weight, and loading instructions when necessary, must be in each aircraft at time of original certification and at all times thereafter.

NOTE 2. The following placards and/or markings must be prominently displayed in the cockpits in full view of the pilot:

    (a) "This airplane approved in restricted category for aerial photography only."

    (b) "This airplane must be operated within the limitations set forth in BUAER PILOTS HANDBOOK AN 01-85FD-1 except for limitations specifically called out in F.A.A. Type Certificate Data Sheet AR-32, in which case values in Data Sheet must be observed."

    (c) "Do not exceed 288 m.p.h. (250 knots) IAS with oil cooler shutter open."

    (d) "Do not extend or retract landing gear at speeds in excess of 160 m.p.h. (140 knots) IAS."

    (e) "Avoid prolonged operation below 25 in.Hg. in normal mixture. Operation below 25 in.Hg. is normal exceeding approximately two minutes may cause the engine to cut-out."

    (f) "When cranking the AEC lever must not be advanced more than 1/3 of its travel. Otherwise the resulting large surge of uncontrollable power can create a hazard."

GRUMMAN F8F-2
TYPE CERTIFICATE DATA SHEET NO. AR-32     November 23, 1959     Page 2

NOTE 3. Prior to civil certification the following must be accomplished:

    (a) Provide oxygen for pilot if airplane is to be operated above 10,000 ft.

    (b) Ascertain compliance with Department of Navy service changes 56, 60, 62, 81, 90, 110, and 135.

NOTE 4. Use of droppable type fuel tanks is permitted provided they are permanently fixed to the aircraft and not capable of being dropped in flight.

··· END ···

Page two of AR-32 giving "Serial nos. eligible for Type Certification, (121523 through 122708)." Certification basis "for the special purpose of aerial photography." Note "No aircraft may be produced under this approval."

Page three of AR-32 stating all Navy service changes must be complied with and the use of droppable type fuel tanks is permitted if they are fixed permanently to the aircraft .

OPERATIONS LIMITATIONS

MAKE            :   GRUMMAN
MODEL           :   F8F2
SERIAL NO.      :   1216 08
REGISTRATION NO.:   N-7700 C

This aircraft has been certificated under the provisions of Part 8 for the special purpose of aerial photography operations.

The aircraft shall not be operated in any manner that will endanger public life and property. The operator shall adjust the take off weight to provide a safe margin of performance for the existing operating conditions, considering the take off area, altitude, temperature and terrain.

Maneuvers shall be limited to those normally performed in aerial photography.

Persons and cargo shall not be carried for compensation or hire.

Persons other than the minimum crew necessary for aerial photography operations shall not be carried during these operations.

No persons shall be carried in the aircraft unless a seat and safety belt, installed in accordance with good aeronautical practice is provided for his use.

Reg. 4 LA
ASDO 20

Airworthiness Inspector
F. A. A., GSDO 4-20 Long Beach
November 4, 1959

FORM ACA-500 (PART B) (3-56)

Form Approved
Budget Bureau No. 41 - R889.4

U. S. DEPARTMENT OF COMMERCE — CIVIL AERONAUTICS ADMINISTRATION

## APPLICATION FOR REGISTRATION

NAME AND ADDRESS OF APPLICANT (Same as that shown on Part A of this form)

Grover Collins
Hacienda Hotel
Bakersfield Calif.

REGISTRATION NO.

N- 7700C

AIRCRAFT MAKE AND MODEL

Grumman F8F-2

CHECK WHETHER OWNERSHIP IS

☑ CORPORATION  ☐ PARTNERSHIP  ☐ CO-OWNERSHIP  ☐ INDIVIDUAL OWNER

SERIAL NO.

121608

I HEREBY CERTIFY that the above described aircraft is not registered under the laws of any foreign country, that the owner whose name(s) appear hereon as the applicant is (are) a citizen of the United States as defined in Section I (13) of the Civil Aeronautics Act of 1938; and that both copies of Part A and a copy of Part B of Form ACA-500 and legal evidence of ownership were forwarded to the Civil Aeronautics Administration, Washington, D. C.

SIGNATURE OF APPLICANT (IN INK)

(If executed for co-ownership, all must sign)

July 5 1958

TITLE    President

DATE OF APPLICATION

I, the above statements are true and made in good faith, the aircraft described above may be operated, pending registration or notification from the Civil Aeronautics Administration, provided airworthiness requirements of applicable Civil Air Regulations are complied with.

FORWARD THIS COPY TO WASHINGTON — Retain Duplicate Copy.

*Left*: Letter from FAA Airworthiness Inspector on November 4, 1959, for c/n D.982, N7700C, detailing "operations limitations." Note that "Maneuvers shall be limited to those normally performed in aerial photography."

*Above*: Application for registration by Grover Collins for c/n D.982, BuNo 121608, as N7700C, to the FAA on July 5, 1958.

The certificate of registration reproduced reads:

FORM ACA-500 (PART A) (3-56)

UNITED STATES OF AMERICA

DEPARTMENT OF COMMERCE— CIVIL AERONAUTICS ADMINISTRATION

## CERTIFICATE OF REGISTRATION

| NATIONALITY AND REGISTRATION MARKS | MAKE AND MODEL OF AIRCRAFT | AIRCRAFT SERIAL NO. |
|---|---|---|
| N- 7700C | Grumman F8F-2 | 121608 |

NAME OF OWNER: Grover Collins

ADDRESS OF OWNER—NUMBER AND STREET: Hacienda Hotel

CITY: Bakersfield, California     ZONE     STATE

It is hereby certified that the above described aircraft has been duly entered on the register of the Civil Aeronautics Administration, Department of Commerce, United States of America, in accordance with the Convention of International Civil Aviation dated 7 December 1944, and with the Civil Aeronautics Act of 1938, as amended, and regulations issued thereunder.

DATE OF ISSUE:

FOR THE ADMINISTRATOR OF CIVIL AERONAUTICS

Robert C. Forbes

CHIEF, AIRCRAFT & AIRMAN RECORDS BRANCH

December 3, 1958 cw

(OVER)

*Above*: Certificate of registration issued to Grover Collins for c/n D.982, BuNo 121608, N7700C, issued December 3, 1958.

*Right*: FAA form-337 showing work completed on c/n D.982, N7700C, to comply with AR-32 by Acme Aircraft.

The FAA form-337 reproduced reads:

## INSTRUCTIONS

This form must be completed in duplicate each time a major repair and/or alteration is made of an aircraft, airframe, power-plant, propeller or appliance. After the repair and/or alteration has been inspected and item 6 completed, the original copy of this form will be made available to the aircraft owner for retention as part of the aircraft records. The duplicate copy is retained by the CAA for administrative purposes.

See CAM 18 for detailed instructions concerning the information to be furnished with this form and instructions concerning its preparation.

8. DESCRIPTION OF WORK ACCOMPLISHED.*

THIS AIRCRAFT WAS MODIFIED TO CIVILIAN STATUS IN ACCORDANCE WITH CAR, PART No. 8 FOR THE PURPOSE OF AERIAL PHOTOGRAPHY IN ACCORDANCE WITH ACME AIRCRAFT COMPANY'S DRAWINGS, DATED 6/20/59 AND PHOTOGRAPHS NOS. 1000-1 and 1000-2 BY THE INSTALLATION OF A FAIRCHILD K-21 AERIAL CAMERA. THIS ESSENTIALLY IS REPLACING THE CAMERA IN THE SAME LOCATION IT WAS WHILE THE SHIP WAS IN MILITARY SERVICE, FOR EXAMPLE JUST FORWARD IN THE MANHOLE SHOOTING IN A DOWNWARD VERTICLE POSITION AND IS ACTUATED THROUGH A MASTER SWITCH ON THE LEFT SIDE OF THE INSTRUMENT PANEL AND TRIGGERED BY THE MACHINE GUN SWITCH ON THE CONTROL STICK. THE AIRCRAFT WAS WEIGHED AFTER THE INSTALLATION OF THIS CAMERA SO NO FURTHER COMPUTATIONS ARE NECESSARY.

*** END ***

*If additional space is needed attach additional sheets bearing aircraft nationality and registration mark and date work completed.

Check block if additional sheets are attached. ☐

This form must be completed in duplicate each time a major repair and/or alteration is made of an aircraft, airframe, power-plant, propeller or appliance.   After the repair and/or alteration has been inspected and item 6 completed, the original copy of this form will be made available to the aircraft owner for retention as part of the aircraft records.   The duplicate copy is retained by the FAA for administrative purposes.

See CAM 18 for detailed instructions concerning the information to be furnished with this form and instructions concerning its preparation.

**8. DESCRIPTION OF WORK ACCOMPLISHED.***

1. Recovered control surfaces and flaps using razorback method approved under S.T.C. SA2-952 following instructions manual 39-5.
2. Removed fuselage drop tank shackle and hardware.
3. Removed armor plates.
4. Removed arresting gear hook and system including catapult hooks.
5. Removed armament switches and wiring.
6. Removed gunsight computer system and harness.
7. Removed all radio controlls except ARC-1.
8. Removed all boxes, brackets, and useless projecting parts from cockpit.
9. Installed map case on right side of cockpit in old radio rack space.
10. Relocated voltage regulator and mount.
11. Moved battery and installed extra heavy duty battery in parallel AT 154.75". Both batteries are mounted on supporting structure attached to fuselage structure similar to original installation. Wire used is same size as original installation. Wire meets MIL Spec. MIL-W-5086. Batteries are vented with neutrilizing jar in vent line.
12. Moved K35 Camera to 169.75" and mounted camera to be serviced by persons designated by owner.
13. Fabricated mounting supports and brackets and installed 42 gal. Timm emergency fuel tank at 99.50"(THIS FUEL TANK INSTALLATION IS AWAITING S.T.C. APPROVAL AND IS NOT TO BE USED OR SERVICED WITH FUEL UNTIL APPROVAL IS COMPLETED).
14. Aircraft was weighed with fuselage main fuel tank full. Radio was removed at time of weighing. Weights are with tare removed.

WEIGHT AND BALANCE

| ITEM | WEIGHT | ARM | MOM. |
|---|---|---|---|
| Left main | 4010 | 9.87 | 39578.70 |
| Right main | 3920 | 9.87 | 38690.40 |
| Tail | 796 | | 168401.76 |
| | 8726 | | 246670.86 |
| Removed Fuel | − 1080 | 55.25 | −59670.00 |
| | 7646 | | 187000.86 |
| + radio | 47 | 104.50 | 4911.50 |
| | 7693 | | 191912.36 |

$$\frac{\text{TOTAL MOM.}}{\text{TOTAL WGT.}} = \frac{191912.36}{7693} = 24.94 \quad \text{empty C.G.}$$

Emergency fuel tank is disconnected and must remain disconnected pending engineering approval or be removed within 90 days.

Typical FAA form FAA-337 for "Major repairs and/or alteration of an aircraft, airframe, power plant or appliance." This shows the type of work carried out to civilianize an F8F-2.

---

## INSTRUCTIONS

This form must be completed in duplicate each time a major repair and/or alteration is made of an aircraft, airframe, power-plant, propeller or appliance.   After the repair and/or alteration has been inspected and item 6 completed, the original copy of this form will be made available to the aircraft owner for retention as part of the aircraft records.   The duplicate copy is retained by the CAA for administrative purposes.

See CAM 18 for detailed instructions concerning the information to be furnished with this form and instructions concerning its preparation.

**8. DESCRIPTION OF WORK ACCOMPLISHED.***

This aircraft has been converted to civilian status

in accordance with Civil Air Regulations and Aircraft Spec. AR-32 by the

installation of a K-24 Camera, in accordance with Acme Aircraft Companys'

data in accordance with the Federal Aviation Agency Fourth Region Engineering.

............................................

Second page of FAA form FAA-337 for c/n D.963, BuNo 121589, N5171V, dated March 15, 1960.

UNITED STATES OF AMERICA
FEDERAL AVIATION AGENCY

## CERTIFICATE OF AIRWORTHINESS

**1. NATIONALITY AND REGISTRATION MARKS**

N6821D

**2. AIRCRAFT AIRWORTHINESS CLASSIFICATION**

EXPERIMENTAL – Exhibition –Racing
(See Reverse Side)

**3.** This Certificate of Airworthiness is issued pursuant to the Federal Aviation Act of 1958. The aircraft identified hereon is considered airworthy when maintained and operated in accordance with the Civil Air Regulations and applicable aircraft Operation Limitations.

**4.** This Certificate will remain in effect as long as the aircraft is maintained in accordance with Part 43 of the Civil Air Regulations unless surrendered, suspended, revoked, or a termination date is otherwise established by the Administrator of the Federal Aviation Agency. THIS CERTIFICATE EXPIRES SEPTEMBER 24, 1965.

**5. DATE OF ISSUANCE**

9/24/64

**6. FAA REPRESENTATIVE**

Charles R. Taylor

**7. DESIGNATION NO.**

CE-GADO-14

**8.** Any alteration or misuse of this Certificate is punishable by a fine of not exceeding $1,000 or imprisonment not exceeding 3 years, or both.

GPO : 1959 OF—508938

Form FAA 1362B (5–59)

*Above*: Example of Certificate of Airworthiness for an "experimental classification" for c/n D.1181, BuNo 121787, N6821D, for the purpose of "exhibition racing" granted to M. W. "Lee" Fairbrother.

*Right*: Page one of the "Experimental Operating Limitations" for c/n D.1181, N6821D, issued by the FAA.

---

Central Aviation District Office No. 14
6301 –34th Avenue South
Minneapolis, Minnesota 55450

### EXPERIMENTAL
### OPERATING LIMITATIONS

| | | | |
|---|---|---|---|
| AIRCRAFT | : Grumman F8F-2 | ENGINE | : Pratt & Whitney |
| REGISTRATION NO. | : N6821D | SERIAL NUMBER | : P-29565 |
| OWNER | : M. W. Fairbrother | PROPELLER | : Aero Products A642-64 |
| | FairAcres, Rosemount, Minn. | | |

This aircraft has been issued a certificate in the Experimental Airworthiness Classification for Exhibition and Racing. The following limitations (restrictions) will apply.

**EXHIBITION:** This purpose pertains to the public display of aircraft at air shows, meets, fairs and other similar gatherings to exhibit the aircraft's flight capabilities. The necessary operation to maintain flight proficiency and travel between points are included under this purpose.

**RACING:** This purpose authorizes the aircraft to be flown in races which are officially sanctioned by the Professional Racing Pilots Association, The National Aeronautic Association or other similar groups. Practice flights preparatory to such racing and flights to and from racing events are included under this purpose. Note: (All practice flights for low altitude (below 1500 feet) racing shall be conducted in an approved flight test area under the terms of a separate waiver.)

1.  The initial flight must be conducted within an approved flight test area. Exit and entry flights from the base of operation to the flight test area are to be conducted within a corridor which is a part of the flight test area.

    (a) The operator must demonstrate that the aircraft is controllable throughout its normal range of speed and performance of maneuvers to be executed and that the aircraft has no hazardous operating characteristics or design features.

    After the above has been completed to the satisfaction of the Administrator and certified to by the applicant, the aircraft may be authorized to operate outside the flight test area in accordance with the following operating restrictions.

2.  Cargo shall not be carried for compensation or hire.

3.  All flights shall be conducted to avoid areas having heavy air traffic and to avoid operation over cities, towns, villages, congested areas or any other area where the flight would create hazardous ex posure to persons or property on the ground.

4.  Operation of this aircraft over foreign countries is not authorized, unless prior permission is granted by the government of the foreign country or countries over which the operation of the aircraft is to be conducted.

5.  Any major changes to this aircraft shall invalidate this certificate.

6.  Flights limited to day and night VFR.

7.  Flight tests are prohibited.

8.  All flights shall be conducted in compliance with FAA Air Traffic Rules.

9.  Operation of this aircraft shall be limited to persons who have full knowledge of the airworthiness status of this aircraft.

10. These Operation Limitations are a part of the airworthiness certificate and shall be carried in the aircraft at all times.

11. The placard "Experimental" shall be prominently displayed at the entrance to the aircraft and visible from the outside.

12. If defects are found or malfunctioning experienced, it shall be immediately reported to the nearest FAA District Office.

Charles R. Taylor
General Maintenance Inspector
CE-GADO-14 Minneapolis

Date:  9/24/64

Expiration Date:  9/24/65

---

UNITED STATES OF AMERICA
DEPARTMENT OF TRANSPORTATION — FEDERAL AVIATION ADMINISTRATION
### SPECIAL AIRWORTHINESS CERTIFICATE

| | | | |
|---|---|---|---|
| A | CLASSIFICATION: | Experimental | |
| | PURPOSE: | Racing and Exhibition | |
| B | MANU-FACTURER | NAME N/A | |
| | | ADDRESS N/A | |
| C | FLIGHT | FROM N/A | |
| | | TO N/A | |

| | | |
|---|---|---|
| D | N— 148F | SERIAL NO. 121787 |
| | BUILDER  Grumman | MODEL  F8F-2 |
| E | DATE OF ISSUANCE  September 12, 1969 | EXPIRY  September 12, 1970 |
| | OPERATING LIMITATIONS DATED  9/12/69 | ARE A PART OF THIS CERTIFICATE |
| | SIGNATURE OF FAA REPRESENTATIVE | DESIGNATION OR OFFICE NO. |
| | ROBERT H. BECKLEY  Robert H. Beckley | GADO 4-2-04 |

Any alteration, reproduction, or misuse of this certificate may be punishable by a fine not exceeding $1,000 or imprisonment not exceeding 3 years, or both. THIS CERTIFICATE MUST BE DISPLAYED IN THE AIRCRAFT IN ACCORDANCE WITH APPLICABLE FEDERAL AVIATION REGULATIONS.

FAA FORM 8130-7 (3-69) SUPERSEDES FAA FORMS 1362-B; 8100-3; 8130-5     *SEE REVERSE SIDE*

*Left*: Page two of limitations for c/n D.1181 in September 1964 and which would expire in September 1965.

*Above*: "Special Airworthiness Certificate" in the Experimental Classification for Racing and Exhibition for c/n D.1181, BuNo 121787, N148F issued to Bud Fountain, who raced it as Race # 99 and #24. It was written off during the Mojave Air Races on October 20, 1973.

FORM ACA-800 (PART C) (7-58)

U. S. DEPARTMENT OF COMMERCE—CIVIL AERONAUTICS ADMINISTRATION

**BILL OF SALE**     178700

For and in consideration of $ ___1.00 and other valuable considerations___ the undersigned owner of the full legal and beneficial title of the aircraft described as follows:

AIRCRAFT MAKE AND MODEL

Grumman F8F2

DOC. RECORDED

SERIAL NO.     REGISTRATION MARKS

Bureau #121776     N—1030B

JAN 22  2 50 PM '60

does this __30th__ day of __December__ 19__59__  FEDERAL AVIATION AGENCY
hereby sell, grant, transfer, and deliver all of his right, title and interest in and to such aircraft unto:

*(Name and address of purchaser—same as on Parts A and B of this form)*

The Kaman Aircraft Corporation
Bloomfield
Connecticut

and to ___their___ executors, administrators, and assigns, to have and to hold singularly the said aircraft forever, and certifies that same is not subject to any mortgage or other encumbrance except

| TYPE OF ENCUMBRANCE | AMOUNT | DATE |
|---|---|---|
| None | | |
| IN FAVOR OF | | |

In testimony whereof I have set __my__ hand and seal this __30th__ day of __December__ 19__59__

NAME OF SELLER ___TRANSAIR, INC.___

BY (SIGN IN INK) ___Robert B Meyer___
*(If executed for co-ownership, all must sign)*

TITLE ___Treasurer___
*(If signed for a corporation, partnership, owner, or agent)*

**ACKNOWLEDGMENT**

of ___New Jersey___

County of ___Union___

On this __30th__ day of __December__ 1959 before me personally appeared the above named seller, to me known to be the person described in and who executed the foregoing bill of sale, and acknowledged that he executed the same as his free act and deed, and, if said bill of sale that of a corporation swore that he was duly authorized to execute the same. Given under my hand and official seal the day and year written above.

(SEAL)

NOTARY PUBLIC OF NEW JERSEY

MY COMMISSION EXPIRES DEC. 12, 1969

MY COMMISSION EXPIRES ___ NOTARY PUBLIC

FORWARD THIS COPY TO WASHINGTON — Retain Duplicate Copy.

Bill of Sale from Transair Inc for c/n D.1161, BuNo 121776, N1030B, to Kaman Aircraft Corp for the consideration of $1.00 and OVC on December 30, 1959. Bearcat was ferried to Bloomfield, CT, for use as a wind machine and did not fly again until March 2003, 44 years later after restoration, as N68RW.

---

WILLIAM M. FULLER
2408 CONTINENTAL LIFE BUILDING
FORT WORTH, TEXAS
76102

July 2, 1970

Mr. Lester G. Robinson
Chief, Aircraft Registration Branch, AC-250
Department of Transportation
Federal Aviation Administration
P. O. Box 25082
Oklahoma City, Oklahoma  73125

Re: AC-259
Gruman F8F-2, Serial 121699

Dear Sir:

Receipt is acknowledged of your letter dated June 30 about the cancellation of U. S. Registration of the above described aircraft. You request that each co-owner must sign the attached AC Form 8050-73. More specifically, you request that Shelby Kritser sign that form.

Mr. Kritser died in the crash which destroyed this plane which occasioned my request for the cancellation of the registration.

Yours very truly,

William M. Fuller

WMF/ks
Enclosures (2)

Letter from William M. Fuller to the FAA about cancelling the registration for c/n D.1073, BuNo 121699, N7826C, after the FAA requestede the signature of co-owner Shelby Kritser to complete the cancellation paperwork.

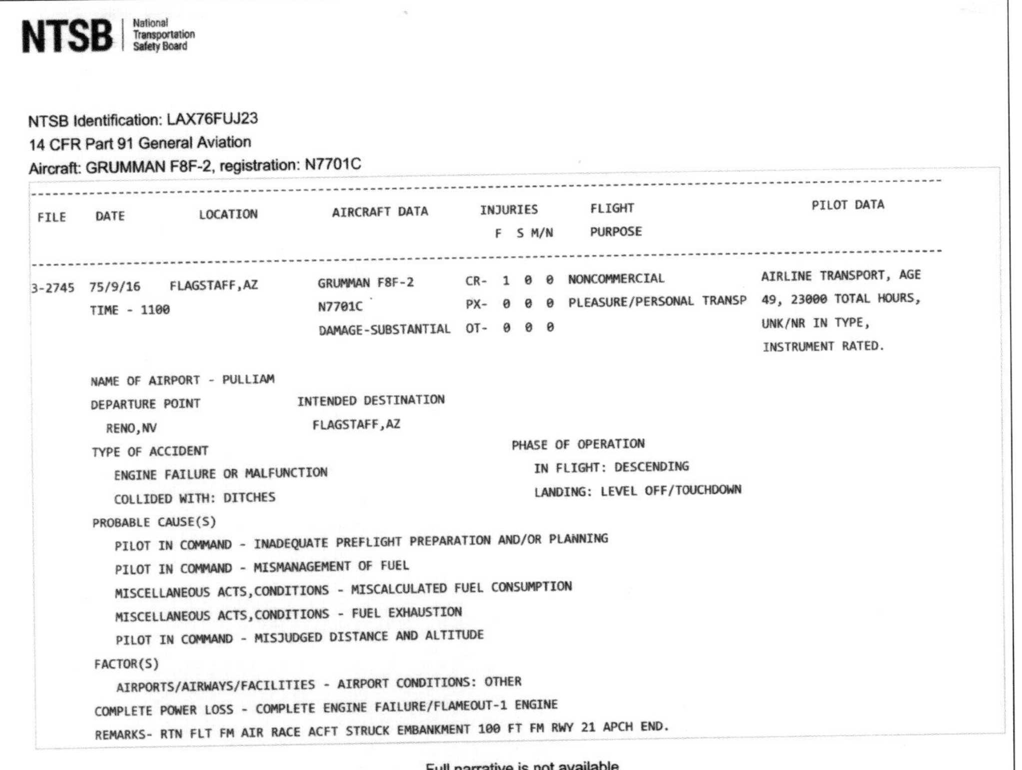

**NTSB** National Transportation Safety Board

NTSB Identification: LAX76FUJ23
14 CFR Part 91 General Aviation
Aircraft: GRUMMAN F8F-2, registration: N7701C

| FILE | DATE | LOCATION | AIRCRAFT DATA | INJURIES | FLIGHT | PILOT DATA |
|---|---|---|---|---|---|---|
| | | | | F S M/N | PURPOSE | |
| 3-2745 | 75/9/16 | FLAGSTAFF,AZ | GRUMMAN F8F-2 | CR- 1 0 0 | NONCOMMERCIAL | AIRLINE TRANSPORT, AGE |
| | TIME - 1100 | | N7701C | PX- 0 0 0 | PLEASURE/PERSONAL TRANSP | 49, 23000 TOTAL HOURS, |
| | | | DAMAGE-SUBSTANTIAL | OT- 0 0 0 | | UNK/NR IN TYPE, |
| | | | | | | INSTRUMENT RATED. |

NAME OF AIRPORT - PULLIAM

DEPARTURE POINT          INTENDED DESTINATION
  RENO,NV                  FLAGSTAFF,AZ

TYPE OF ACCIDENT                         PHASE OF OPERATION
  ENGINE FAILURE OR MALFUNCTION            IN FLIGHT: DESCENDING
  COLLIDED WITH: DITCHES                   LANDING: LEVEL OFF/TOUCHDOWN

PROBABLE CAUSE(S)
  PILOT IN COMMAND - INADEQUATE PREFLIGHT PREPARATION AND/OR PLANNING
  PILOT IN COMMAND - MISMANAGEMENT OF FUEL
  MISCELLANEOUS ACTS,CONDITIONS - MISCALCULATED FUEL CONSUMPTION
  MISCELLANEOUS ACTS,CONDITIONS - FUEL EXHAUSTION
  PILOT IN COMMAND - MISJUDGED DISTANCE AND ALTITUDE

FACTOR(S)
  AIRPORTS/AIRWAYS/FACILITIES - AIRPORT CONDITIONS: OTHER
COMPLETE POWER LOSS - COMPLETE ENGINE FAILURE/FLAMEOUT-1 ENGINE
REMARKS- RTN FLT FM AIR RACE ACFT STRUCK EMBANKMENT 100 FT FM RWY 21 APCH END.

Full narrative is not available

*Above*: Copy of NTSB report LAX76FUJ23 on the accident involving c/n D.1261, BuNo 122708, N7701C, that was the last F8F-2 Bearcat built.

*Right*: The Bill of Sale for c/n. D.1033. Note the re-typed BuNo and registration number.

FORM ACA-500 (PART C) (3-56)

U. S. DEPARTMENT OF COMMERCE — CIVIL AERONAUTICS ADMINISTRATION

## BILL OF SALE

For and in consideration of $ 1650.00 the undersigned owner of the full legal and beneficial title of the aircraft described as follows:

| AIRCRAFT MAKE AND MODEL | |
|---|---|
| Grumman – Model F8F-2 | **N4993V** REGISTRATION MARK |
| SERIAL NO. **S/N 121859** Bureau No. 122659 | |

does this 4 day of December 19 58, hereby sell, grant, transfer, and deliver all of his right, title and interest in and to such aircraft unto:

(Name and address of purchaser—same as on Parts A and B of this form)

MADDEN & PLAYFORD AIRCRAFT INC
5353 N.W. 36 St.
MIAMI 48 FLORIDA

and to his executors, administrators, and assigns, to have and to h singularly the said aircraft forever, and certifies that same is not subject to any mortg or other encumbrance except

| TYPE OF ENCUMBRANCE | AMOUNT | DATE |
|---|---|---|
| NONE | | |
| IN FAVOR OF | | |

In testimony whereof we have set our hand and seal this 4th day DECEMBER 19 58

NAME OF SELLER  ACME AIRCRAFT PARTS INC

BY (SIGN IN INK) Louis Walter
(If executed for co-ownership, all must sign)

TITLE  PRESIDENT
(If signed for a corporation, partnership, owner, or agent)

### ACKNOWLEDGMENT

State of CALIFORNIA

County of Los ANGELES

On this 4th day of DECEMBER 19
before me personally appeared the ab
named seller, to me known to be the per
described in and who executed the forego
bill of sale, and acknowledged that he executed the same as his free act and deed, o
if said bill of sale be that of a corporation swore that he was duly authorized to exec
the same. Given under my hand and official seal the day and year written above.

NOTARY PUBLIC

MY COMMISSION EXPIRES
My Commission Expires Nov. 24, 1962

(SEAL)

FORWARD THIS COPY TO WASHINGTON — Retain Duplicate Copy.

# Chapter 7

# TABLES

Lewis Fighter Fleet F8F Bearcats. (Jay Miller)

**Table 1: Construction numbers (c/n) to Bureau of Aeronautics Serial Numbers (BuNo) to Civil Registration Numbers (N#). Registrations are in order of application. Flight status correct at time of publication.**

| Construction number | Model | BuNo | Registration(s) | Flight status |
|---|---|---|---|---|
| D.10 | XF8F-1 | 90446 | N99279, NL14HP | HVY-DMG remains stored |
| D.18 | XF8F-1 | 90454 | N6624C, N3351, N9G | FLIES |
| D.527 | F8F-1 | 95255 | N65135, N41089, N58204 | FLYABLE |
| D.628 | F8F-1 | 95356 | N7247C, N4752Y | FLYABLE |
| D.739A | G-58A | NONE | NC1201V, NL3025 | W/O 01/18/1949 |
| D.779 | F8F-1B | 122095 | G-BUCF, N2209 | FLIES |
| D.902 | F8F-2 | 121528 | N9886C, N212KA | W/O 12/12/1968 |
| D.963 | F8F-2 | 121589 | N5171V, N5555H | W/O 04/18/1967 |
| D.982 | F8F-2P | 121608 | N7700C | W/O 06/05/1971 |
| D.988 | F8F-2 | 121614 | N7957C, N747NF | FLYABLE |
| D.1020 | F8F-2 | 121646 | N7699C, N1111L | DISPLAYED |
| D.1053 | F8F-2 | 121679 | N4992V, N818F | RESTORATION |
| D.1073 | F8F-2 | 121699 | N7826C | W/O 08/13/1966 |
| D.1081 | F8F-2 | 121707 | N1027B, NL3025 (2) | FLIES (as c/n 739A) |
| D.1088 | F8F-2P | 121714 | N4995V, N1YY, N700H, N700HL, G-RUMM | FLIES |
| D.1105 | F8F-2 | 121731 | N1028B, N500B, N5005 | W/O 07/18/1971 |
| D.1122 | F8F-2 | 121748 | N1029B, N618F, N200N, F-AZRJ, N224RD, N1DF | FLIES |
| D.1125 | F8F-2 | 121751 | N9885C | W/O 06/18/1980 |
| D.1126 | F8F-2 | 121752 | N7827C, N2YY, N800H | FLIES |
| D.1148 | F8F-2 | 122619 | N7958C, N700F, N14WB | FLIES |
| D.1162 | F8F-2 | 121776 | N1030B, N68RW | FLIES |
| D.1171 | F8F-2 | 122629 | N1031B, N777L | STORED |
| D.1181 | F8F-2P | 121787 | N6821D, N148F | W/O 10/20/1973 |
| D.1190 | F8F-2 | 122637 | N1033B, N198F, N8TF | FLIES |
| D.1201 | F8F-2 | 122648 | N1032B | W/O 10/09/1960 |
| D.1227 | F8F-2 | 122674 | N7825C | RESTORATION |
| D.1258 | F8F-2 | 122705 | N4989V | SCRAPPED 02/09/1961 |
| D.1261 | F8F-2 | 122708 | N7701C | W/O 09/16/1975 |
| D.1262 | G-58B | NONE | N700A | FLIES |

## Table 2: Civil Registrations to Bureau of Aeronautics Serial Numbers to Construction Numbers.

| Registration number | BuNo | Construction number | Model |
|---|---|---|---|
| N1DF | 121748 | D.1122 | F8F-2 |
| N1YY | 121714 | D.1088 | F8F-2P |
| N2YY | 121752 | D.1126 | F8F-2 |
| N8TF | 122637 | D.1190 | F8F-2 |
| N9G | 90454 | D.18 | XF8F-1 |
| NL14HP | 90446 | D.10 | XF8F-1 |
| N68RW | 121776 | D.1162 | F8F-2 |
| N14WB | 122619 | D.1148 | F8F-2 |
| N148F | 121787 | D.1181 | F8F-2P |
| N198F | 122637 | D.1190 | F8F-2 |
| N200N | 121748 | D.1122 | F8F-2 |
| N212KA | 121528 | D.902 | F8F-2 |
| N224RD | 121748 | D.1122 | F8F-2 |
| N500B | 121731 | D.1105 | F8F-2 |
| N618F | 121748 | D.1122 | F8F-2 |
| N700A | NONE | D.1262 | G-58B |
| N700H | 121714 | D.1088 | F8F-2P |
| N700HL | 121714 | D.1088 | F8F-2P |
| N700F | 122619 | D.1148 | F8F-2 |
| N747NF | 121614 | D.988 | F8F-2 |
| N777L | 122629 | D.1171 | F8F-2 |
| N800H | 121752 | D.1126 | F8F-2 |
| N818F | 121679 | D.1053 | F8F-2 |
| N1027B | 121707 | D.1081 | F8F-2 |
| N1028B | 121731 | D.1105 | F8F-2 |
| N1029B | 121748 | D.1122 | F8F-2 |
| N1030B | 121776 | D.1162 | F8F-2 |
| N1031B | 122629 | D.1171 | F8F-2 |
| N1032B | 122648 | D.1201 | F8F-2 |
| N1033B | 122637 | D.1190 | F8F-2 |
| N1111L | 121646 | D.1020 | F8F-2 |
| NC1201V | NONE | D.739A | G-58A |

| Registration number | BuNo | Construction number | Model |
|---|---|---|---|
| N2209 | 122095 | D.779 | F8F-1B |
| NL3025 | NONE | D.739A | G-58A |
| NL3025 (2) | 121707 | D.1081 | F8F-2 |
| N3351 | 90454 | D.18 | XF8F-1 |
| N4752Y | 95356 | D.628 | F8F-1 |
| N4989V | 122705 | D.1258 | F8F-2 |
| N4992V | 121679 | D.1053 | F8F-2 |
| N4995V | 121714 | D.1088 | F8F-2P |
| N5005 | 121731 | D.1105 | F8F-2 |
| N5171V | 121589 | D.963 | F8F-2 |
| N5555H | 121589 | D.963 | F8F-2 |
| N6624C | 90454 | D.18 | XF8F-1 |
| N6821D | 121787 | D.1181 | F8F-2P |
| N7247C | 95356 | D.628 | F8F-1 |
| N7699C | 121646 | D.1020 | F8F-2 |
| N7700C | 121608 | D.982 | F8F-2P |
| N7701C | 122708 | D.1261 | F8F-2 |
| N7825C | 122674 | D.1227 | F8F-2 |
| N7826C | 121699 | D.1073 | F8F-2 |
| N7827C | 121752 | D.1126 | F8F-2 |
| N7957C | 121614 | D.988 | F8F-2 |
| N7958C | 122619 | D.1148 | F8F-2 |
| N9885C | 121751 | D.1125 | F8F-2 |
| N9886C | 121528 | D.902 | F8F-2 |
| N41089 | 95255 | D.527 | F8F-1 |
| N58204 | 95255 | D.527 | F8F-1 |
| N65135 | 95255 | D.527 | F8F-1 |
| N99279 | 90446 | D.10 | XF8F-1 |
| F-AZRJ | 121748 | D.1122 | F8F-2 |
| G-BUCF | 122095 | D.779 | F8F-1B |
| G-RUMM | 121714 | D.1088 | F8F-2P |

## Table 3: Assigned Race Numbers.

**DNQ** = DID NOT QUALIFY, **DNR** = DID NOT RACE, **DNS** = DID NOT START, **ENT** = ENTERED

| Race # | Registration | Aircraft name | Model | BuNo | Race | Pilot(s) | Other race # |
|---|---|---|---|---|---|---|---|
| 1 | N1111L | GREENAMYER BEARCAT, SMIRNOFF, CONQUEST 1, AMERICAN JET SPECIAL | F8F-2 | 121646 | RENO 1964–71, 1975, BOULDER CITY 1965, LANCASTER 1966, MOJAVE 1975 | DARRYL GREENAMYER, RICHARD LAIDLEY (R-72) | |
| 4 | N7701C | ESCAPE II | F8F-2 | 122708 | RENO 1973–75, MIAMI 1973, MOJAVE 1974–75 | JACK SLIKER | |
| 7 | N618F | | F8F-2 | 121748 | RENO 1966 DNQ-DNR, MOJAVE 1971 | BUTCH MORRIS | |
| 7 | N9G | ROTO-FINISH | F8F-1 | 90454 | RENO 1969–70, TRANSCON 1969–71, MOJAVE 1970, CAPE MAY 1971 | GUNTHER BALZ | |
| 8 | N7827C | SWEET P | F8F-2 | 121752 | RENO 1972–73 | JOHN HERLIHY | 10, 8, 106 |
| 8 | N800H | PRECIOUS BEAR | F8F-2 | 121752 | RENO 1977, 1980–81, HOMESTEAD 1979 | DON WHITTINGTON, BILL WHITTINGTON (R-1980–81) | 10, 8, 106 |
| 10 | N7827C | MATHEWS BEARCAT, TOM'S CAT, MISS PRISS | F8F-2 | 121752 | RENO 1964–69, 1971, BOULDER CITY 1965, LANCASTER 1966, TRANSCON 1968 (ENT-DNS) 1969 | WALT OHLRICH, SANDY FALCONER (R-1966) | 8, 106 |
| 11 | N148F | CHURCH BEARCAT | F8F-2 | 121787 | TRANSCON 1967 (ENT-DNR) RENO 1966–67 | CHUCK KLUSMAN (R-1966) JOHN CHURCH | 24, 99 |
| 14 | N14HP | KIMBERLY BROOKE | F8F-1 | 90446 | RENO 1984–98, 2003–09, BAKERSFIELD 1985, HAMILTON 1988, SHERMAN 1990, WATKINS 1990, DENVER 1992, OLATHE 1993, PHOENIX 1994–95 | HOWARD PARDUE | |
| 23 | N14WB | TEMPUS FUGIT II | F8F-2 | 122619 | RENO 2007 | DAVE MORSS | |
| 24 | N148F | HAWKE DUSTERS | F8F-2 | 121787 | RENO 1973, MOJAVE 1973 | BUD FOUNTAIN | 11, 99 |
| 41 | N9885C | LOIS JEAN | F8F-2 | 121751 | RENO 1973, MOJAVE 1973 | MIKE SMITH | 80 |
| 44 | N5005 | | F8F-2 | 121731 | RENO 1970, SAN DIEGO 1971, TRANSCON 1970 (DNF) | RON REYNOLDS, MIKE GEREN (SD-1971) | 66 |
| 52 | N68RW | BLUE ANGEL #1 | F8F-2 | 121776 | RENO 2011 DNQ | NELSON EZELL | |

| Race # | Registration | Aircraft name | Model | BuNo | Race | Pilot(s) | Other race # |
|---|---|---|---|---|---|---|---|
| 66 | N5005 | | F8F-2 | 121731 | MOJAVE 1970 | RON REYNOLDS | 44 |
| 70 | N777L | ABLE CAT | F8F-2 | 122629 | RENO 1969 | LYLE SHELTON | 77 |
| 77 | N777L | ABLE CAT, PHOENIX 1, PHAST PHOENIX, 7½ PERCENT SPECIAL, OMNI SPECIAL, AIRCRAFT CYLINDER SPECIAL, RARE BEAR | F8F-2 | 122629 | RENO 1970–75, 1980–81, 1983, 1985–92, 1994–97, 1999, 2003–15, MOJAVE 1973–76, SAN DIEGO 1971, CAPE MAY 1971, MIAMI 1973, BAKERSFIELD 1985, HAMLITON 1988, PHOENIX 1994–95 | LYLE SHELTON, JOHN PENNY (R-1985–87, 1994–96, 2003–05, 2007–10, STEWART DAWSON (R-2011–15), MATT JACKSON (R-1999), RON BUCCARELLI (R-2006) | 70 |
| 80 | N9885C | MISS SMIRNOFF | F8F-2 | 121751 | RENO 1964–65, BOULDER CITY 1965, LANCASTER 1965 | MIRA SLOVAK | 41 |
| 98 | N198F | CHURCH BEARCAT, HERLIHY BEARCAT | F8F-2 | 122637 | RENO 1972, 1978–79, MOJAVE 1971 | JOHN CHURCH, JOHN HERLIHY 1978–79 | |
| 99 | N148F | | F8F-2 | 121787 | RENO 1969 (DNQ-DNR) | BUD FOUNTAIN | 24 |
| 99 | N212KA | KUCERA BEARCAT | F8F-2 | 121528 | TRANSCON 1968, RENO 1968 | ROBERT KUCERA | |
| 106 | N800H | WAMPUS CAT | F8F-2 | 121752 | RENO 1998–99 | WILLIAM ANDERS | 10, 8 |
| 204 | N41098 | | F8F-1 | 95255 | RENO 1996–99 | DAVID PRICE (R-1996), ALAN PRESTON | |
| 224 | N224RD | BLUE BEAR | F8F-2 | 121748 | RENO 2007 | RAY DIECKMAN | |
| | N818F | | F8F-2 | 121679 | AT RENO IN 1967 DNQ-DNR | | |
| | N1033B | | F8F-2 | 122637 | AT RENO IN 1969 DNQ-DNR | | |

Grumman F-14D Tomcat, Model G-303, BuNo 164604 was the last Tomcat for the United States Navy with VX-9. It was the last fighter aircraft built by Grumman in a line that started with the FF-1, which was the only fighter aircraft equal to the F8F Bearcat. Both are "The Last of the Red Hot Cats." (Craig Kaston)